Y0-DOS-939

Give Thanks

By
Lyn Brickles

Second Edition

To JOHN & FAMILY

WITH BLESSINGS

Lyn B

Give Thanks
Copyright © 2015 by Lyn Brickles. All rights reserved.

No part of this publication may be reproduced, stored in a retrieval system or transmitted in any way by any means, electronic, mechanical, photocopy, recording or otherwise without the prior permission of the author except as provided by USA copyright law.

The opinions expressed by the author are not necessarily those of Tate Publishing, LLC.

Published by Tate Publishing & Enterprises, LLC
127 E. Trade Center Terrace | Mustang, Oklahoma 73064 USA
1.888.361.9473 | www.tatepublishing.com

Tate Publishing is committed to excellence in the publishing industry. The company reflects the philosophy established by the founders, based on Psalm 68:11,
"The Lord gave the word and great was the company of those who published it."

Book design copyright © 2015 by Tate Publishing, LLC. All rights reserved.

Published in the United States of America

ISBN: 978-1-68118-596-5
1. Biography & Autobiography / General
2. Biography & Autobiography / African American & Black See Cultural Heritage
15.04.01

GIVE THANKS

With a Grateful Heart
By Lyn Brickles

Memories of a life on three Continents.

"Let me tell you a story".

"TO MY PEOPLE"

This book would not have been possible without a great deal of help from

Jerry and Kathie Roberts – Scribe & Interpreter

BB – Comptroller

Kevin Ortega – Facilitator

With the sincere appreciation of "The Producer".

INDEX

ENGLAND

Winkle Street, Calbourne, Isle of Wight

Heritage

The River Thames rises in the Cotswold Hills in Gloucestershire and flows through the home counties until it comes at length to London, then south east to the English Channel. At it's southern reaches the river becomes tidal as it hurries to join the sea.

A "Cockney" is a title given to persons who are known to have been born in the east end of London and within the sound of the Bells of the Church of St Mary Lebow – "Bow Bells", and the rest of us tykes are <u>just</u> Londoners.

"Mudlark" is a Londoner's nickname for someone born "on the banks" of the River Thames – not literally of course – but at least adjacent to the river and within the Greater London area. My mother informed me that I was born in a house on a street next to the Thames in Chiswick – which made me a Gen – u –wine Mudlark.

I always had an affinity with the river and between the ages of 10 and 16 I spent very many happy hours on the banks and in the water of the Thames. There must have been 6 or 7 of us in "Our Gang" and most of those were boys including my brother, Brian, and our expeditions were legend on our street. Those were the early years of WWII and our excursions were restricted to bus or bicycle rides – so our horizons were only bounded by the pennies in our pockets and the strength in our skinny legs.

We had such good times – packing up bread and jam "sarnies", mixing bright yellow lemonade crystals with water in large thick glass bottles for a lipsmacking picnic.

We'd catch the bus for a tuppenny ride to Twickenham and troop down the lane to the ferry landing, where for a penny each the ferryman would row us around the end of Eel Pie Island and over to the towpath on the far bank of the Thames at Mortlake. Inevitably this motley crew couldn't land without scuffles and differing opinions on the direction we should take up or down stream.

Up stream was Teddington Locks and Runnymede and further on Hampton Court, Windsor, Maidenhead and Henley – on – Thames.

Down stream the river glided past Richmond and the famous KewGardens, Chiswick and on through London past Greenwich, to the south coast and the channel.

All the upstream points were our playground. Very early spring and summer weekend mornings would see 4 or 5 of us mounting our junk yard bikes and setting off on a day long trip up river. We rode swam, laughed and fought all day long like the puppies we were – all this during a World War on our doorsteps. We distanced ourselves from all that to some degree, pushing away reality, but the wailing of air raid sirens often insinuated that dreaded noise into our hours of play. We were far from shelter out there but not fearful.

Sometimes we lay, with damp, goose bumped skin, on the grass of the river bank and watched the dog fights in the sky overhead, cheering on our heroes in their tiny Silver Spitfire and Hurricane Aircraft as they fought up there to keep the enemy from our skies.

This was the time of the "Battle of Britain" about which Winston Churchill coined his historic phrase – "Never in the history of human conflict has so much been owed by so many to so few"

I think Runnymede was one of our favourite spots, it lay between Staines and Old Windsor and the river here ran easily between the old historic Water Meadows where the Magna Carta was signed in the year 1215. No tow paths there and we would camp (that usually meant everything was dropped where we stood) then we would dare each other to swim across the river. Of course they knew I would -- I was a pushover for a dare. The boys had no choice – they had promised to look after me.

I can picture them still in my minds eye, Pat Lucas, tall and wiry with dark wavy hair and flashing black Latin eyes, girls fell for him all the time and he hated it – <u>Well</u> he did <u>then</u>! I was immune to his charms and anyway I was almost a boy so I didn't embarrass him.

Next was "Bobo" Birch and his brother Eddie, Bobo got his nickname because he did such a great imitation of a Chimpanzee – prancing and grunting around and scratching his arm pits.

Tubby Rice was another of our crew, his given name was Terry, but he was a very large boy – I mean big and overweight. Kids can be cruel, so came his nick name Tubby.

Jackie Jones, what can I say about Jackie Jones, well mine were the googoo eyes of puppy love, to me he was perfect in every way. I suspect that my daring escapades were an effort to get his interest - - - - it didn't work.

On the other hand BoBo thought I was great – how do I know? Well he told me so! – That's life – even those early years had their little romantic heartaches – but there was never any hanky-panky.

So we were all water babies – splashing and laughing, just being so innocent and happy in our own way.

We swam the Thames at Twickenham and dangerously at Teddington Locks, at Runnymede and we tried to at Henley-on-Thames. But fussy grounds keepers and stewards chased us away, probably for fear that we might mess up the pristine site of the famous Henley Regatta.

I'm sure our comments must have been pithy and very insulting.

So all things pass and become memories – eventually the war ended and we outgrew our trips – most of us were working after the age of 14, there was no further education for us. No more play time, the sun set and adulthood beckoned.

But I'm still a Mudlark and a Londoner –
That's my Heritage.

A Village Easter Memory

Great Horwood is a very old English Village, set in the County of Buckinghamshire, N/west of London.

The village snuggles comfortably against green soft bosomed hills and serenely watches the centuries pass.

Viewed from a distance there was no set pattern to the houses that comprised Great Horwood. Apart from the fringe of cottages around the Village Green most of the dwellings lay scattered like alphabet blocks tipped from a toy sack. They seemed to have settled higgledy piggledy where they fell.

Rough stone walls lichen encrusted, in colours shading from saffron yellow, thro' silvery grey to deep, funereal purple! encircled the ancient church yard. Many of the tombstones are so old and weathered that the inscriptions have become illegible.

Set into the floor of the nave in the greystone church are the tombs and memorials of Knights, Squires and their ladies from days of old. They are depicted on great bronze panels wearing full armour, holding swords and complete with a small dog at their feet.

A steady trickle of art students and visitors came to the tiny church to kneel, -- not in prayer – but to take brass rubbings of these raised surfaces, and so to spread our history out of the village.

On a Saturday, at Easter every year, a village fete was held (at Great Horwood) the actual event was not sited in the village proper but in the grounds of the Manor House, home of the local squire and his family for generations.

The mildewed skeletons lying beneath your feet within the church were probably direct ancestors of the squire and the house lands and tenants were also inherited, passed from eldest son to eldest son.

Set in spacious grounds a ½ mile west of the village, Horwood House was a red brick Regency building (unspoiled by additions).

Just a nice 3 storied, 18 room dwelling – whose down to earth red brick glowed rosily in the evening sun, in those days. When I was 7 (seven) yrs old, all the days were summer – or so it seemed.

The fete was a special event, because the squires lady, as president of the village chapter of the "Women's Institute," involved all her "ladies" in the work and planning.

A large marquee would be erected and all sections of competitive events would be held within- arts and crafts, cookery, preserving etc.

From many estate barns where they had rested since last years August flower show, were brought forth the trestles and forms. These crudely crafted tables would be erected around the front lawn of the manor forming a rough circle around the tent.

They would be manned (or should I say wo-manned) by ladies of the Women's Institute. Some were volunteers, but most were press-ganged into service. I tell you not many refused to help "the squires lady", husbands and sons worked on the estate, and glad of it in those days.

On the day, the tables would display all that the squires lady, had managed to chivvy and dredge up from her sources, merchants in local towns and society friends. There was a white elephant stall holding the cast out treasures someone bought here last year, and crafts ranging from carving, sewing, knitting and crochet to woodwork.

Buy some raffle tickets for a suckling pig who sat in a wooden pen squealing for his mummy. Try to guess the weight of a large jar of beans and win a laying Rhode Island Hen.

From a stall at the far side refreshments were sold, glasses of homemade lemonade, pasties and ginger bread slices. Right next door a "nice cuppa tea" was dispensed from a large shiny urn whose leaky tap never seemed to get fixed from year to year.

The tea, served in thick white "institution" style cups, was mixed with milk from a huge enamel jug that took both hands to lift and pour.

Generous spoonfuls were dipped out of a large china basin of sugar that had little balls of brown tea drop clustered sugar atop it from wet tea spoons. The trick was to get your sugar with no brown balls in it- that took time causing the serving ladies to chivvy you along, "stop mucking about you young'uns".

For the children two things were of prime interest, the clown in lavish paint and gaudy costume, his comical antics and free balloons were a big draw.

The other thing was the discreetly placed striped Romany tent, it sat in a corner quiet and mysterious yet drawing, attention like a poultice. The "young'uns" watched like hawks for the young girls, who would nudge and cajole one another into spending a precious few pennies on "Gipsy Rosalie's" fortune telling skills.

This was all ammunition for a few days of teasing and cat calling about "what the Gipsy told them" about their love lives or whatever their salacious little minds could conjure up – just to annoy - young brothers were a squirrelly lot!!

The marquee tent, bulging with goodies in many catagories, and also with sturdy country bodies, was a steam bath. Heat was not the only pressure within there, hopes and prestige were at stake and many a hanky was twisted in sweaty fingers awaiting the judges verdicts. Never mind! There's always next year!!

The day wore on, and a small Brass Band came toward evening from the town of Winslow and gave a concert of pomp and circumstance music, Edward Elgar was a rural favourite and so patriotic.

Dusk came, the uninvolved wandered home to supper and the volunteers set to and cleared all the paraphernalia away, the tables and tents and venerable tea urn, all to be stored until the flower show in August on the Village Green.

The Squire and His Lady slipped away up to "The House" for a much needed "G&T" or glass of Sherry and breathed easier because it hadn't rained and the day seemed to be a success.

Tomorrow, Sunday, was church and on Monday the estate gardeners would set to and repair the manor lawn for another year.

Easter was over – Great Horwood settled back onto it's comfy couch and waits for summer and another century to roll by.

We are all Blest

God gave us eyes and someone taught us to read and understanding came with practice.

Autodidact is a good word and it describes me. But I digress – Best loved childhood books was the subject and as an octogenarian I can lay claim to having read about a million books during my life so far.

I say so far because, my motto is press on with the job lads and don't count the empties.

One very early book I read, one of the first to make me cry was "Uncle Toms Cabin." I was seven years old. The story told of life as black people in America's Southern States and the cruelty that was meted out and endured. How could people be so cruel? -- How indeed!! So I cried.

Most of the following years were filled with the age appropriate tomes until I arrived at 9-10 years. Then my education took a decided elevated curve – I wanted to know and understand.

I think I was a sneaky kid, No I'm sure I was – I didn't miss many tricks and when my father, who had an extensive library of thousands of books, proceeded to curtail my permission to browse in there – the question "WHY" cropped up in my devious canny young mind. So I sneaked in and browsed – without permission. Eventually I found out. By dint of a lot of eavesdropping and skulking about I had an idea of why I was being kept out.

My father had spoken to my mum about a copy of a book that was banned and only kept in a brown paper cover, Mum did not seem impressed but her nervous caution piqued my juvenile interest. Now the race was on, could I find and read this book before the hammer (father) fell.

I won't keep you in suspense – I found it and read it – but I didn't understand it – The book was "Lady Chatterley's Lover" – and thus began my AUTODIDACTISM – a form of self education and study. On the bottom shelf of a bookcase at home was housed a huge dictionary so large it must have weighed 5-6 lbs, and this heavy book became my tutor. Did I mention that it was an illustrated dictionary!! There were a great many queries raised in my brain because of the book in the brown paper cover. I had to know!

So this plain little girl, with her pudding basin cut, brown hair got herself educated by reading continuously, repeatedly and obsessively, that old book until the meaning and the spelling of much of the contents were imprinted in her mind. I was eventually a sure choice for spelling bees. Some tutorial heads were shaken at this skill – I did not know any better – I could just spell. Some strange words were used about my English compositions, one word I looked up in the ubiquitous dictionary phonetically – and it was plagiarise. So in conclusion this piece tells of two small books I read before I read the ancient, heavy, illustrated reference dictionary.

Currently I am trying to read again a book by Edward Rutherford, a historical novel on the city where I was born, London. From the age of creation from mud to a truly great place. I'm a Londoner and proud of it.—Does it show?

My Heart's Desire

Lustrous cascades of chestnut hair tumbled to the delicate lace-edged collar of her swiss dotted white dress. White ankle sox and black patent leather strap shoes, the epitome of class and style, completed the ensemble.
Pansy soft brown eyes, framed by long silky lashes, gazed out upon the world with an air of royal condescension. A delicate pale complexion with a hint of blush on the cheeks and soft pouting pink lips seemed to issue a never-ending siren call to be kissed.

I had gazed upon this beauteous apparition for what seemed like months, but in fact she had only moved onto our area recently – and there was I, a slight, fidgety seven-year-old with dark eyes in a sun-browned homely face framed by brown hair fashioned into a "pudding basin" cut, and I was in love, head over heels, for the first time.

My Mum was the only one I could talk to about my obsession. She worked miracles every day – I heard my Dad say so.

The words did not come easily for me and I knew Mum had a lot on her plate with my sickly baby brother needing her constant attention. But I plunged into my story and then sat waiting for her to speak.

When I raised my eyes I saw tears coursing down her face and dashed to wipe them away with my ever-grubby hands. Sorry to have made her *cry and* woken up the baby.

"Oh Bubby," she said, "how can I explain that some things can't be changed and that you have to accept gratefully what you get in this world."

My heart's desire seemed beyond my reach and I tried hard not to yearn after "Beauty," but seven-year-old hearts and brains to not easily accept reality. They still believe in miracles.

December first arrived crisp, cold, and snowy. The cold air in my bedroom made cartoon balloons of my breath as I grabbed my clothes in a bundle and ran downstairs to the warm kitchen to dress in front of the kitchen range.

There on the table were a pile of letters and a large brown paper parcel all for me. Carefully I untied the white string and then pulled frantically at the brown paper to reveal – a homemade rag doll!

Not until I was a mum myself trying to fulfill, with limited means, the hopes and dreams of my own children did I truly appreciate my mother's gift of hours spent making my birthday present.

The "Beauty" disappeared from the window of the corner toy shop in time to become another little girl's Christmas doll, and with her went my heart's desire – at least for *that* year.

BEGGARS CAN BE CHOOSERS

Circumstances determined the migration of the Byrne family, my parent's, Brother Brian and me from bucolic starvation in the country to a similar situation in the City of London, district of Paddington.

Spring of 1936 I was 8 yrs. old and a tenement in "Conduit Mews" was our new home – one large room, scullery and shared facilities.

Father found work but it was on location outside London and meant time away. Mum became a "nippie", a waitress at one of "Lyons" Teahouses, but that was shift work.

During the days our parents slogged away Brian and I – well really just me found new avenues of entertainment, country joys like fishing for tadpoles and tiddlers in the brook or picking blackberries for jam were fast fading from our country bumpkin minds.

Tenements are renowned for teeming with kids, like cockroaches they seem to be there and Conduit Mews was no different, the kids came tumbling out of the concrete stairways and boy did they have all the angles covered. Cutting a long story short – I joined a gang.

Now some youngsters are able to adapt to new situations fairly easily but Brian was fragile – an injury at birth had affected his motor and speech skills.

As a result of our parent's schedules we were left alone quite a lot and especially I was reminded that as a big girl looking after my brother was my main job.

I felt at times that he was permanently attached to my left hand – why left hand you wonder – I simply needed my right hand to fight with. His stammer and draggy leg made him a butt for bullies and jokers and someone had to put 'em right.

A granny who lived in the basement was recruited and paid to watch out for us now and again, but when "fun' could be heard in the mews I was gone with the wind.

"The Gang" were denizens of the mews – all boys, none over 12 yrs. old and their street smarts were second nature. They could earn money in so many ways my parents had to be kept in the dark.

All hardened smokers of the "filfy Woodbine" and drinkers of amazing quantities, in large glass bottles of "Tizer", at the time "Tizer" was England's Coca Cola.

Money to pay for these items of luxury and indulgence was earned in many different ways, -- but nothing illegal, we were just self interested juvenile entrepreneurs.

When the open fronted Greengrocers and Dealer Grocery stores closed up for the night and pulled down the shutters, they put out the trash for the daily early morning pick up by the council dustmen/trash collectors. As soon as the last lock latched and last light dimmed inside the store the "urchins" were there turning over the trash looking for treasure.

Most Greengrocers and some Grocers received deliveries in wooden boxes in those days, from South Africa banana and orange boxes – those were a prize for me – you could make furniture out of orange boxes. Grocers had eggs delivered in wooden crates, also tea chests from India were at premium. In all this frantic searching we had a strict rule – leave no mess – tidy it all up – because the Bobbie on his beat and the store owner would soon put a stop to our "Game".

Our "Game" was to take all the wooden boxes down a quiet alley and with our boots smash them on the kerb side to make kindling. From outside the "United Dairy" shop were usually some cardboard boxes or used string bags in which we carefully measured out quantities of kindling sticks and these were then touted down to the kitchen basements of the Bayswater and Kensington upper class houses, priced at a reasonable penny or tuppence according to quantity – to the cook/housekeeper or maid, we invariably made a profit – those big houses had many fireplaces besides the kitchen cook stove, but we only called twice a week and never did we deliver in another wooden box { I only did it once }, if there were no cardboard boxes or string bags we wrapped the kindling in newspaper.

Towards the Bayswater Road, on Spring Street there were two popular, posh restaurants and one nightclub – Friday and Saturday evenings would find some of us, who could get out, lurking around the corner or in a nearby doorway waiting for a taxi to draw up and deposit his fare. Usually a couple or party of four would alight and up front and center would appear two "urchins" – 1st opens the taxi door and greets the people, 2nd opens restaurant or club door whilst also extending hand for a small tip. Once I got a whole sixpence! WOW. I bet that was a mistake on that young Toffs part.

But we could only do this if the premises did not employ a doorman to do that job, dodging trouble was the name of the game and so to borrow a small phrase from "somewhere" we were artful dodgers.

The spoils, tips, earnings etc. were shared out and had to be hidden or spent – how could we explain the cash!

Now and again we offered to do jobs for shopkeepers, like the greengrocer. He sometimes needed cleanup help before closing up and we got paid in "specky" fruit and old wilting veg, not a bad deal, veggie stew was a staple where we lived, and running "errans" for people in the neighbourhood – sometimes we even did it for free, especially for grannies, they didn't want much –some milk from the dairy - pinch of tea from the grocers or a jug of stout or ale from the off license at the pub. We'd trot along with the jug and come back with two pennyworth of "juice that's good for what ails you"!!

Now and again we did healthy things, like going for rambles – a couple of jam sarnies and a bottle of "Tizer" for picnic supplies and we would set off for Kensington Gardens and the round pond, just for fun.

Brian would be attached to my left hand as usual, he loved these adventures, especially if – for a change, Mum knew what we were doing – what can I say – the kid had a conscience!!

We may have been streetwise beggars but also so naive as not to assimilate most of the evil in the world around us and unaware at that moment in time, 1937/38, of the sickness at work in Europe that would turn our worlds into fearful chaos.......World War 2.

Sunday Morning

On a sunny and bright Sunday morning in early September my brother Brian and I set out from our home on our weekly "Duty Call" on Granma and Granpa Carroll. Not for us the dreaded Sunday school with its wax crayons and stiff sheets of drawing paper waiting with baited breath to receive our unskilled artwork of the Bible stories. No! We must visit Layton Road where our grandparents lived.

Arrayed in our "Sunday Best" clothes, we received the usual admonitions from Mum of "don't spill anything down your front and keep your fingers off your sides" we set off, leaving her to prepare dinner and Dad glued to the Wireless Set.

Lacking a certain eagerness in our step, we paced the mile and a half to Granma's house.
Generally known as "A Tarter" Granma Sue was a roly poly little lady, about 5 ft. tall but with a tongue like a whiplash, she had delivered and raised eleven children and although my Granpa was a retired Royal Marine Sergeant Major, Granma Sue was his equal when it came to discipline (and I was a challenge – always)

Granpa Albert was another reason I was so wary of these visits mainly because we were expected to give him a kiss on arrival, which was fraught with danger. Granpa wore a huge military moustache – plus he smoked an everlasting pipe and his moustache bristles painted a generous dollop of nicotine onto tender cheeks. As a result we wiped and rubbed our faces from the irritation and were chided for our bad graces and lack of manners. "rubbin your granpa's kisses off indeed". We couldn't win for losing plus I wasn't allowed to answer back so you can imagine what a chore it was to visit Granma's.

On this Sunday Granpa was unusually close by his wireless set – like Dad. As a rule Granpa had by now had his usual prairie oysters and left for the British Legion Veterans Club to work up an appetite for Sunday Dinner – roast beef and Yorkshire pudding.

On this Sunday Granma didn't keep us long and early ushered us on our way with further warnings "not to muck about" on our way home.

We left to dawdle home, just 9 yr old Brian and me, soon to be eleven. The big 11 plus exams were coming up at school next and I knew my scores would rule where my education would proceed from there, Grammar School or Secondary Modern, and I "sort of" worried.

As we ambled along a procession of Army Lorries and a couple of Army dispatch riders on motor bikes passed along the road and over the hump backed bridge that crossed the railway lines.

We had just passed over the top of the bridge hand in hand because the Army Convoy had made us nervous – when suddenly the most awful sound in the world exploded around and into our ears – an awful relentless wailing sound, so loud we couldn't think.

Terrified I started to bolt for home pulling an equally frightened Brian with me. Not six paces later I tripped on a raised paver and fell down hill dragging my brother with me.

Poor Brian smacked his eyebrow on the pavement and immediately started bleeding and screaming, in complete panic I tried to lift him up but he was down.

Then I saw that I had knocked a great chunk from my left knee and the blood was running freely down my leg to my lovely white ankle sox. All the time that awful noise continued to terrify us.

Suddenly over the hump backed bridge roared an Army motor bike dispatch rider, he must have miscalculated his speed and the height of the road because he crashed on landing and left himself unconscious on the roadway with the bike sliding sideways down the hill beside us.

What chaos for two kids on their way home from Granma's!

Soon other Army personnel and policemen, were on the scene and we finally got home for our Sunday dinner, hysterical, bloodied and bruised. Later the reasons for the Military Convoy were explained.

The date was Sunday 3rd of September 1939 and Britain on that day declared war on Germany!! The beginning of WWII.

The noise? Well that was the sound of an Air Raid Siren to which we became forever fearful.

Brian still has a scar on right eyebrow!

Mrs. Poole's Cupboard

"Come on, best foot forward," my Mother's voice seemed to echo from the farthest reaches of my memory, and my right foot slid reluctantly over the threshold of the boxlike structure before me.

Someone, obviously more eager than I to board this contraption, gave me a none-too-gentle nudge in the back, forcing me to advance further into a state of incipient panic. A gentle flutter started in the pit of my belly – I tried to ignore it.

Turning to face the front and striving to control the squirrel of crazy images racing round and round in my mind, I took a deep breath to try to conquer my fear, and I watched mesmerised as the heavy doors of the lift slid silently, relentlessly, together.

A slight tremor of movement travelled up my legs to join the flutter in my belly, and my hands clasped each other as though fearful that one would manage to slip away and desert me, or signal my fear.

My eyes focused with desperate urgency on the indicator over the closed doors, waiting for No. 3 to show up, and so release me from purgatory.

For many years I was only aware of slight discomfort in enclosed places, such as changing booths in dress shops, in milling crowds, and of course, lifts. Until the last few years, when in search of good stories to tell, I brought back sensations of fear when my memory touched upon a certain period of my childhood. So I became brave and chased fear back, and this is a piece of that story.

I was eleven years old three months after England entered World War II on September 3rd, 1939. With my parents and younger brother, Brian, I lived in an upstairs flat in the Greater London Area of Hounslow. Brian and I attended the same school, Chatsworth Junior, and I was in the last year of study to take my 11-Plus Exams. These exams were a big deal then, supposed to point your future and path in life. Future became a moot point from then on, in the prevailing circumstances.

Almost immediately after war was declared the Army took over part of our school, and there, to the great excitement of the children, they parked armoured cars and tanks in our playground. It was the call up of regiments of the Terrier, the Territorial Army, equivalent to the U.S. National Guard.

For almost a year following the outbreak of war different units of the Army occupied our school, and the education of the pupils suffered mightily. The Junior School had to share the smaller Infants School facility on half days only, so we went to school at midday to enlarged classes, with most of the male teachers gone to war.

Not only did the Army annex our playgrounds as parking lots for military vehicles, our playing fields, of happy cricket, soccer, and hockey memory, were desecrated to the gods of war and used to construct underground air raid shelters for our protection from the bombs of the *enemy.*

Well, amazingly, we contrived to assimilate our new lifestyle of part-time education and part-time parents, absent on shifts in aircraft factories as mine were. They went to help manufacture the means of bombing other peoples' children – but those people *were* the *enemy,* were they not???

In late 1940 I failed my 11-Plus Exams, most of which were taken in the air raid shelter, and moved to the

Bulstrode secondary modern school which was situated mid-town, about a three-mile walk from home.

As if ordained, my three years at Bulstrode heralded the start of *The Blitz*. The dreaded Luftwaffe of old Nasty Adolf commenced to blast England and London in particular, with nightly bombing raids. Used as we had become to the daytime raids, nighttime raids were truly terrifying. As I mentioned earlier, our family lived in an upstairs flat. There were just the two floors, and the folks who lived beneath us on the ground floor were Mr. and Mrs. Poole and their teenage daughter, Mavis.

As is the manner of Londoners, they offered to share the comparative safety of the downstairs kitchen during the worst raids. They had a Government-issue indoor air raid shelter which consisted of a six-foot-square, table-like structure made of sheet steel, with strong wire mesh welded around the sides leaving a three-foot opening at the front. Into this metal cave were placed mattresses, bedding, and as many bodies as possible.

Both men had work that kept them away at night. Claude Poole was a railway policeman, and Paddy Byrne, my Dad, worked night shift in the aircraft factory. My Mum was on the day shift. On most nights Mrs. Poole and Mavis shared the shelter with Mum, Brian, and me.

Needless to say I became the body they least wanted to share this confined space with. In retrospect, the betting could go on *some* wanting to send me out into the night to take my chances – but they were good people and sorely tried.

I won't go into details of my anti-social behaviour, but suffice it to say that *ultimatums* were issued, and I had become tagged as Adolf's Secret Weapon – they could put up with the air raids, but me in the table shelter was too much already.

So a plan was devised. The front stairs to our upper dwelling made a nice cupboard underneath in the Pooles' flat called – surprise – "The Cupboard under the Stairs." Placed in here were the meters to record the gas and electricity consumption, which were visited every three months by official meter men to read them for billing purposes. It also contained an assorted jumble of tennis rackets, hockey sticks and boots, and Mr. Poole's fishing rods and tool boxes.

So – this was my fate – I must sleep under the stairs – in the Cupboard. Now the Blitz proved, and subsequent earthquakes and tremors too, that one of the safest places was under the stairs, but I did not want to be a *good* girl and go quietly into, what I termed, the *coffin*.

You know, I think that twelve-year-olds of that era were so much younger and more malleable than has since become the norm. They were told to mind their manners, give older people and pregnant ladies the seat on the bus, and obey parental requests. *Not me!* Someone had to be the exception to the rule and I was it. Oh not in minding my manners, but a Mississippi mule must have found its way thro' my Irish ancestry and settled its stubbornness into me.

Herr Hitler swung the pendulum against me and fear made me crawl into my nest of blankets under the stairs, but not without pleading cries of, "Please – *Please* Mummy, don't shut the door." It all comes tumbling back to me, of waking to the floor heaving under my body, and the awful noise of the next high explosive bomb whistling its way down to find *me – and the door was shut!!!*

That still makes me break out into a sweat when I recall it, and it was repeated for many months. We would go to school in the morning's thro' streets choked with rubble and cough on the acrid smoke of the burning goods and homes of our neighbours, and sometimes of the people themselves.

Strange, isn't it, that we never turned into mass murderers or psychos because of the trauma of all those years, early childhood years, having to cope with daily and nightly imminent death. We were all those skinny kids, near the bone because of the stringent food rationing – with our one-parent families – no-parent families when the call went out for night and day shifts to win the war – we became the original *Latch Key Kids.*

But the era of psychology and psychiatry had not yet conditioned us to think of ourselves as victims of our circumstances.

So I think that one of my legacies from those war years may be an irrational fear of enclosed spaces and crowds. The closing of the lift doors triggers a fear I cannot control, but I pretend it doesn't exist, and hope that no one notices that I have regressed to the times in Mrs. Poole's Cupboard and a child's voice crying – "Please – *Please* Mummy, don't shut the door!"

Wartime Easter Outing

The fare on the No.33 big red double-decker bus was a penny a mile and half price for children. From Whitton Road to the other side of Richmond Bridge was six miles so the cost was six pence (6 cents) for adults and thrupence (3 cents) for children and the adventure was worth every penny.

My Mum was the one who took us, my brother, Brian, and me on occasional outings, and a springtime trip on the bus of Richmond-on-Thames on a Sunday afternoon was a rare treat. We children would wait eagerly at the bus stop at the end of our street for the bus to appear on the road over the far railway bridge, vying with one another as to who would get on the bus first and claim the window seat. The betting was always on me as I was three years older than Brian and an accomplished bully!

Once our red chariot arrived we would scramble, pellmell up the metal stairs to the upper deck and if we were very lucky the front seats with their all-round windows would be empty and waiting for us. Such a view you didn't get even riding in a Rolls Royce.

The route went down through Whitton stopping every quarter mile or so to pick up or let off passengers, the double "ding-dong" of the bell telling the driver, marooned in his box like driving cab up front beside the engine, to go on after each stop. Even the metallic ting of the conductor's punch as she made a hole in the ticket as you paid your fare, was part of the outing atmosphere.

Past "Twickers," our famous rugby football ground, and on into Twickenham where the route took a sharp left turn to go south along beside the river Thames.

Marble Hill with its historic house whose park was an accepted public playground and picnic place now, was at one time the regency era trysting place for a once scandalous royal liaison. Do times and people really change, even royalty? I ask myself! Unaware of history, children ran and screamed, played and ate picnics in those lovely surroundings.

Richmond at last, as we rolled across the old stone balustraded bridge we gazed down upon the river, only slightly busy with water traffic. Then a glance up at the hills above the river showed a joyful array of pink and white blossoms and masses of yellow daffodils. It always seemed that every tiny crevice that would give purchase to a spring bulb had been filled.

The town of Richmond, a royal borough no less, rose tier upon tier above the serpentine curves of the river Thames and the view from the terraces above the botanical gardens was truly impressive. One could see way back down river almost to Eel Pie Island, and in April showers the sun gave us some gorgeous rainbows.

For Mum we must visit the botanical gardens and enter, wrinkling our noses, into the musty, damp heat of all the ancient greenhouses. Trying to read the Latin names on labels and being reprimanded for rowdy behaviour – me, not Brian! Mum was dedicated gardener and as it was wartime she had given up her flower garden to "dig for victory" and planted vegetables. To see all the carefully nurtured blooms was probably a balm to her gentle nature.

At last, duty done, we could careen up the terraces and up Richmond Hill to the old Royal Hospital, home to badly injured service veterans of the "First Great World War" (the one to end all wars – remember?). At this time it was rapidly filling with a new crop of casualties from this war – WWII.

Just by the hospital and close to the great impressive ornamental gates into Richmond Royal Deer Park, was a very steep, leafy, stone-stepped lane. It led down to the river meadows where sleek, plump, caramel-coloured Jersey cows chomped contentedly on knee-deep grass that was thick with buttercups and daisies.

The woodlands to the right of the path were lit by masses of bluebells, like a carpet of blue, so deep and true it is difficult to describe, but it is imprinted still on my memory. It was there I was taught one of my first lessons in conservation — don't pick the bluebells – they just die in hot careless little fists.

We turned back along the river bank, feeding the swans from a brown paper bag of bread scraps, past people relaxing in deck chairs on the newly mown lawns at the water's edge.

An ice cream cone from the stand near the bridge was the last treat of the day and we ate them sitting on a bench at the river's side. I love that river because I am a "mudlark" and have a kinship with it.

Now to catch the bus for the return journey, home to bread and jam and maybe cake, and school tomorrow.

Thank you, Mum, for all these indelible, lovely memories; I have thought of Richmond often, in Spring, whilst living in a desert in the middle of Africa and have become so homesick

Let's Have A Nice Cuppa Tea

For most of my life those few words have meant to me Comfort, Sympathy, Caring and Loving. I suppose you could say that many children of my generation were weaned on a "nice cuppa tea" ,and for sure, tea must have been a flavour in our mothers milk.

During WWII we spent many hours in air raid shelters, and I remember huge enameled jugs filled to the brim with glorious, dark brown liquid sweetened by runny spoonfuls of Nestle's Condensed milk. The jugs of tea were brought around the air raid shelters by W.V.S. (Women's Volunteer Services) ladies. All that tannic acid must have helped keep our chins up.

From when I had babies I remember midwives who would clean up and then say, "Now for a cuppa to bring that mother's milk in," and so that they could take a chance to rest their weary feet.

Births , deaths, bad news, good news, tragedy , accidents, and all kinds of calamity were coped with by "a nice cuppa tea". Funny how no one seemed to reach for the brandy or such – just a "cuppa".

Once in Africa a very traumatic thing happened to a dear English friend. She, her husband and visiting daughter and two year old granddaughter were kidnapped at night from inside our compound by armed terrorists , taken in to the Kalahari bush , and dumped there bound hand and foot. Eventually the husband got free and brought the women and child to my door to care for them whilst he tried to get help.

As you can imagine they were in a very bad way ,and, after bathing their poor feet and scratches, I put the kettle on for a "cuppa" – no stimulants, no false props, just love and care and a "nice cuppa tea". They were fine after a day or two.

Now I'm sure you all know how to make tea your way. Let me tell you how my Mum made it. The kettle, filled with fresh cold water, was put to boil. Then out came the tea tray, next the tea caddie containing loose tea leaves (Indian- Ceylon blend), the teapot with its stand, and tea strainer with its own little saucer – next, cups and saucers, teaspoons, milk jug and sugar bowl, and last but not least , the tea cosy.

When the kettle started to sing , about a cupful of hot water was poured into the teapot – and then a timeless ritual took place. With both hands Mum would take the teapot and swirl the water round in the pot a half a dozen times – anti-clockwise! Pouring out the water she would spoon in the tea – one spoon per person and "one for the pot".

Once the water in the kettle came to "rolling boil" (I love that - I credit my daughter , Joy, with that description. She talked to the Christmas Association in 1990/91 about making a cup of tea) – and the rolling boil was poured steadily over the tea leaves in the pot which stood on its stand, lid put in place , followed by the cosy. All was allowed to draw (brew/steep) for five minutes. After about four minutes the tea was stirred vigorously with a teaspoon to help the flavor, then let stand a minute to allow the agitated tea leaves to settle down.

Some time ago I was in an English tea shop , "Lovejoy's " in Florence, on the Oregon coast, where you get your teapot and all the gubbins (etceteras) just like at home. As I stirred the pot, the owner of Lovejoy's remarked in a loud voice "Only an Englishwoman would stir the pot before

she poured". I guess it's like a trademark or "made in "
mark

To continue – Now small amounts of milk were poured
into the bottom of the cups for those who took milk, and
the tea was at last poured into the cups thro' the tea strainer
to catch stray leaves – voila – magic – delicious - ! Nectar
of the gods! A cuppa.!

The seeming ceremony of my Mum's tea making appears
to have vanished with that era – progress gave us electric
kettles. Microwaves, and teabags, etc. and the time it once
took is at a premium.

But my two or three cups of tea in the morning still taste
delicious – I guess you could say "I'm hooked on tea" .
But , I do have one small confession to make. I use tea bags
instead of my traditional English tea leaves, but only
because good tea leaves are so hard to find.

HOIST
Youthful Indiscretions

Having fluffed my lovely white wings and patted my slipping halo to a saucier angle I gave serious consideration to the subject.

After a full five minutes I reached a decision – No Way – put into writing any misdeeds or tall tales from over the years – I don't think so, so little time – so much to tell.

But wait – my first and only encounter with the constabulary – that's a good story.

In wartime England – 1940 or 41 – the bicycle crew – three boys and me plus my little brother Brian who had no bike and rode on some ones crossbar were up for almost anything and fine weather and fewer day time air raids gave us scope during the summer break from school.

Riding our bikes one day along the back path by the railway lines we passed a small area of railway property. A tiny triangle of land surrounded with 6 ft. chain link fencing topped by two strands of rusty sagging barbed wire.

Several enameled signs festooned the fence warning of the punishments for trespassing, as the signs were considered target practice by many boys the message on them was barely legible as the enamel was prone to chipping from the stones and rocks aimed at them.

Among a few other fruit trees on the railway property was a large Greengage tree and at that time of the season the fruit on it hung ripe and heavy, golden and beckoning!

Almost without discussion a raid was set in motion and we – the three boys and I set our bikes against the fence, climbed to stand on our saddles and shimmied over to go scrumping. Brian was left to mind the bikes.

I remember the taste of that forbidden fruit, sweet and juicy and free. The boys were filling their shirts with fruit to take home, I only had on a dress and my navy blue gym knickers, so I started to stuff fruit into them – it must have made me waddle in a very comical way.

Brian was screaming to us from the pathway and a concerted scramble for the fence started. Burdened by the fruit we were not quite as lithe as when we first climbed it and there on the path one large hand holding his own bike by the handlebars and Brian's arm with the other was a large police constable – a Bobby.

Over the boys went pell-mell, grabbed their bikes and were away – fast.

Yours truly waddled up to the fence, I knew I was caught but the voice of authority said "Get over here girl" – I climbed and was nearly over when my bulging Navy blue gym knickers got caught on the barbed wire and left me hanging and stuffed with pilfered fruit and terrified at the thought of what my Dad would say and do.

The constable, an old style bobby, firm but kindly, finally got me unhooked, but he had to let Brian loose to help me and my darling little brother ran home and told on me.

On the policeman's instructions I threw all my ill gotten goods back over the fence and then he marched me home.

I did get beaten – but most hurtful my bike was locked up for a month. I guess you could say I was hoist by my Navy Blue Gym Knickers!

The Carroll's Are Coming
Hurrah, Hurrah!!

My Mother had four Brothers and four Sisters. All of them born into a family of whom the Paternal Head was my Grand Father Carroll who was a Colour Sergeant Major in the "Royal Marines". An illustrious occupation in those far-off days.

An obvious assumption could be that all those children were drilled in their behaviour along Military Lines, and that assumption would be correct – but the matriarch of this brood was the real Martinet. She had to be, a child was born every two or three years from 1906 onwards until there were nine.

My Grandmother, Susan, was five feet tall and almost the same wide and was known (and feared) as a Tarter! A well earned description that she had laboured long and hard to earn.

When my grand parents stood side by side they looked like "Mutt and Jeff" – She short and so plump, brown pansy eyes, rosy cheeked with wispy greying hair pulled up into an inefficient bun atop her head, from which it fought continuously to escape.

Grandpa was a broad six footer with true military bearing. He had sparkling ice blue eyes and as a seemingly necessary accoutrement to his rank, a "Kaiser Wilhelm" moustache, complete with sharp pointed waxed ends. In his hand would be his favourite "meerschaum" pipe, ready filled with the best 'Erinmore" tobacco awaiting an opportunity to escape and puff in peace some where.

I was told several times by my mother, that this very splendid moustache would cause me to scream when I was a baby when he graciously bestowed a kiss upon my tender cheek. The combination of bristle and nicotine must have reacted like acid on that baby skin.

Not surprisingly my grandpa decided his boys would have a military education with a service career following on from it.

So first, 10 year old Albert (Bert) went to the boys Naval Training School at Chatham in Kent.Then, in order of their birthdays, Alfred (Alf), Leslie (Lal) and John-Pat joined a service school. Alf, Lal and John-Pat became Airmen after graduating into the "Young" Royal Air Force.

Crafty old grandpapa! He was a canny parent, he assigned all of his sons teenage years to military discipline and so avoided having to deal with four lusty young bucks who might question his dictates. I'm not sure if they loved him, but respect for his authority was always apparent.

The girls were harder to farm out, the eldest Patricia and next in age Evelyn – my Mum, were sent off into "service" at a large preparatory boarding school for boy, in the wilds of Suffolk. Irene (later known as Bubbles) went her own way and I'm not sure but I believe she went on the stage, anyway she was very glamorous when she visited and she smelled great. In later years she owned and ran a very successful Inn/Hotel.

Thelma became a Nurse and devoted her life to caring for the mentally ill. She was a pussycat and was very kind to me as I grew up and made my youthful mistakes.

Margaret (Peg) was the baby and only six years older that I so we both managed to grow up during WWII.

These uncles and aunts were jolly, joking, opinionated people full of loud laughter and noisy teasing games. To a lonely, bookish young girl they were super beings. They loomed large on my horizons and I loved them dearly, especially the uncles. Uncle Bert gave wonderful rides and swings and Lal could yodel up a storm so that you thought you were in Switzerland.

During WWII both of my parents worked in the aircraft industry on "War Work" as it was called and sometimes both had to work night shift at the same time, on those occasions Brian, my brother and I must stay at Leyton Rd, Grandma's House – (which I hated).

I was convinced that Grandma didn't like me, bet she was of the same opinion, I don't suppose it had anything to do with my bad behaviour? What can I say? She brought out the worst in me! Or was it vice versa?

My uncles were all serving in different war zones, Bert (the Sailor) on board a Battleship – who knows where? Lal and Pat, Both now Pilot Officers in the Royal Air Force were with their squadrons in the Far East. Alf, also a pilot officer in the R.A.F. had been invalided out of the service early in the conflict after a bad plane crash severely injured him.

But soon we counted our blessings – A miracle occurred during the Autumn of 1943, word was received that "The Boys" were going to come home on leave – together !!

Berts' ship had docked at Chatham for repairs after a U-Boat attack. Lal and Pat were home on relocation leave, Lal from India and John/Pat from Burma.

I suspect a great deal of wrangling went on to bring that about.

Such excitement, so much to say, so many questions and jokes and laughter for the Carroll family. It was a great reunion and a lot of pooling of ration books and squeezing of food for a feast out of reluctant grocers must have gone on because "The Tartar" was in charge of the cookhouse.

Maybe even a little black marketeering went on because my Grandpapa had "contacts" at his local hostelry -- nudge, nudge, wink, wink and a finger at the side of the nose!!

I am sure the result of all the finagling was a resounding success, and not a drop wasted or spilled.

The delight of a fifteen year old hero worshipper must have been like a shining light, on the happiness of the whole family who relished "the boys" being home together in the middle of World War II.

All there forbore to use the standard greeting to most service people which was as follows – welcome – when do you go back? We knew they had to go back but praise to the Lord we had them close for a while.

I bet my hero worship got tedious after a couple of days, I know I received enough tips and pennies to go to the cinema for a few hours. Hey! whatever works!

Bert returned to Chatham and the Royal Navy and the Royal Air Force got their top pilots back. The few days break was wonderful for all of us during the war on all our fronts. When they left we reinvested our prayers and hopes for the safe return of "our boy's"!

And they did return safely, and became civvies in the postwar England that they fought for, and set to with all the repairs and restrictions that lasted for a long time after WWII ended in England.

And eventually I too became a service woman in my own right. Alls well that ends well. Amen

Does your Country Need – You?

The drums they boomed, the cymbals clashed, and the brass rang out so grand,

And we banged our heels and swung our arms to a first class military band –

Yes – We – A platoon of 24 girls in a passing out parade of 150 bodies. We – the rag, tag and bobtail that had straggled out of Leicester City Station one afternoon some six and one-half weeks before.

It was mid-August 1946. I was 17 ½ years old, not now so full of the Old Madam attitude I had arrived with, but feeling a quiet pride and confidence instilled in recruits by drill sergeants from time immemorial.

Glen Parva Barracks, Wigston Magna, Leicestershire, in northern England, was a training camp for girls joining the Auxiliary Territorial Service, known during WWII as the A.T.S. The war was just over, but our service in the Army was still on a war footing and we would not be discharged until the "Powers-that-Be" decided hostilities had *really* ended.

What must have been the reaction of the training staff, at the beginning of July, watching our arrival. We must have looked like the pieces of an animated jig-saw puzzle.

Tall ones, short ones, shy and brassy ones, blonde and brown and red-heads, accents from the four corners of the Kingdom – we were all material to be molded into cohesive, trained units able to serve "King and Country" with some degree of competence.

My decision to "join up" had been inspired both by my disappointment with my previous employment and inability to get along with my farther – what can I say – I, too, was a "teenager"! So anything that took me away would be a bonus – especially as I would be learning a trade. Oh, how I wanted to be a driver! And I was sure the Army would teach me to swagger around at the wheel of a ten-ton truck!!! The corporals and sergeants herded us together like sheep being worked by well-trained sheepdogs. One majestically proportioned lady sergeant informed us that she was a Staff Sergeant, and so must she be addressed – after which announcement she proceeded to read a barrage of instructions from her clipboard in a tone of command very alien to our civilian ears.

It transpired that we must deposit our luggage in one of the Army trucks parked in the station yard, and our bodies into the TCV next to it. "TCV – what's a TCV?" came in wails from all sides. "Troop Carrying Vehicles, ladies," roared the Staff Sergeant in totally different tones than those she had used earlier. "Get aboard – *Now!*" We got!!

TCVs are not the easiest of vehicles to board, and to the uninitiated, in our blocky "wedgies" and civvy clothes and tight skirts, it was like scaling Mount Everest – but eventually we were settled – after a fashion – and chattering like magpies.

A voice we would come to recognize and obey instantly cut through the gabble – "Recruits 'tention! These orders will not be repeated so listen and remember – you will proceed to barracks where you will be assigned beds – you will proceed to stores where you will be issued uniform, gear, and bedding. The uniform gear will be stored in your locker and the bed made up. With your platoon NCO you will march to the cook house for the evening meal. Lights out will be a 9:30 p.m., or 2130 hours, and reveille at 5:30 a.m. – Welcome to the Army!"

Suddenly, strangely subdued, we sat on the wooden seats whilst the vehicles set out for Glen Parva Barracks in the village of Wigston Magna.

As the trucks entered the barracks gates we saw *smartly* uniformed women moving *smartly* about and the word *smartly* was one that we would become sick to our back teeth with – but we were still very naive – *naieeve!*

On a great open tarmac area were several groups of girls marching to shouted order, and we marveled. A voice floated up from a group outside a hut – "Abandon hope all ye who enter here – and the Best of British Luck" – where upon the worm of concern wiggled a little jig in our tummies.

We were unloaded in front of a long, low building, and after collecting our small suitcases we entered a foyer on one side of which was a door marked "NCO Room" – but the barrack room, its shining red concrete floor mirroring fifteen iron bedsteads lined at even spaces down each side was what got our attention. Metal cabinets and wooden chests at the bed ends were for gear stowage.

We chose our beds and tried to collapse onto them – but this was not allowed – not the Army way!

In retrospect I look back thro' the years in wonder at those young girls, none much more than 17 ½ - 18 years old, who had survived in a nation beset by a world war on their doorstep – literally.

A myriad of reasons had, like a high tide, lifted them up and deposited them in this situation which would change them from girls into young women of some worth – and they were all volunteers!

Army issue included clothing from the skin out – three of everything – plus bedding and cleaning gear to maintain uniform buttons and shoes. Also one of each:

knife, fork, spoon, and white enamel mug, listed in military jargon as "Utensils – troops, for the use of."

What a culture shock! Of all the uniform items the knickers were the most hated, made of a silky thick stocking-knit material, long legs with elastic at the bottoms which almost reached your knees. Most of us had hysterics at the sight of ourselves in these garments – compulsory attire, we were informed – and they soon got a name that stuck – "Passion Killers."

Not that many of us knew what passion was, there was still a degree of innocence in some of our worlds back then. Most of our impressions were born in the cinema watching flickering celluloid dramas – when we could afford the price of a ticket.

With our "kit" stowed in lockers and chests, we were ushered out, eating utensils in hand, into the evening and told to "form up in three lines and three-abreast." Well, it must have looked like Casey's Court – 24 "Babes in the Woods" trying for the first time to obey given orders.

Eventually, with Corporal Baker, our platoon commander, calling in cadence, Left – right, left – right," attempting to get us all into step, we set off across the parade ground. *What a shower!* We were slip-stepping all the way, which had a hilarious domino effect through the ranks, as our NCO remarked, "More like fox trotting at the 'Palais de Danse' than marching."
We became accustomed to caustic remarks, they were the training staff's stock in trade.

To the cookhouse for our first Army Catering Corps meal, supper of sausages, mash, baked beans, and great wedges (doorsteps) of bread and margarine. There were mugs of very dark, sweet tea and an apple for dessert.

Then we went slip-sliding our marching way back to our quarters to finish settling in.

Lights out was right on the dot of 9:30 p.m., or 2130, and I went to sleep to the sound of whispered conversations and someone nearby quietly crying.

05.30 a.m. reveille was a complete culture shock, and, after hurried ablutions, trying to dress in the new uniforms caused a great deal of dismay – who knew from tying ties? But our Corporal Baker, who slept in the small room off the entrance, helped, chivvied, and taught us how to wear and care for our uniforms, a whole new world of "polish shoes and polish buttons" opened up ominously before us.

Whilst ministering to us, the corporal continued to issue streams of instructions on Army protocol, thus:

- No running in barracks, unless in dire emergency.
- March *smartly* always.
- No hair on or below collars, put it up or cut it.
- No makeup for period of training.
- No pass outs until three weeks into training.
- Obey all commands without question.
- Learn to use military time, e.g., in 100 hours.

The last two items I failed to accomplish continuously during my two and one-half years service.

On this second day of training we were given full medical and F.F.I. (Free From Infection) exams, had two inoculations, and were issued our pay books, our only I.D. from now on. We were instructed to learn our Army Number by heart. No pay was issued until you identified yourself to the paymaster by rank, number, and name.

Mine was: Private – W/338435 – Byrne – *Ma'am!* Once learned, never forgotten!

Our poor, daffy young brains reeled with the barrage of do's and don'ts, all interspersed with Corporal Baker teaching the right way to make our beds, and then how to "barrack" them for daily inspections. "Barracking" your bed meant folding sheets inside folded blankets, and then stacking them with extreme precision at the foot of your bed on top of your three straw-filled "biscuits" which made up your mattress. Your pillow sat atop the lot.

Many a tear was shed before the required degree of precision was attained, and this applied not only to "barracking" one's bed, but also recognizing officers and saluting them all the time, and learning to march. These were all high on the list of things to attain.

Hoo! Boy! Was I a dilly! Our drill sergeant, Sergeant Major Evans, was from the Welsh Guards. Six feet, three inches of solid, loud, *do as I say* voice, he also had ears that could pick up and locate a whispered comment from 50 paces away.

Strangely, once you get the rhythm of swinging arms and legs properly, it was almost hypnotic – at least it was to me. So much so that one day when he made me Right Marker leading the platoon, I reached the far side of the barrack square before I realized I was alone. Sergeant Major Evans had called, "Squad Right Turn," and everyone did –but me! I got three days of one-hour drill after supper as punishment, and he made me Right Marker for many more sessions to make me lead the platoon correctly. Thus I learned to listen. But here also was born my love of marching, and rousing brass band music.

My story began with our passing out parade, the triumphant culmination of six weeks of extremely hard work and training, not only by us girls, but by the professional training corps of NCOs and officers at this camp.

This was our proudest day, and marching back and forth on that parade ground completing our drills with crisp precision, all to the stirring sound of a band of the Welsh Guards, was an unforgettable experience. Most of us were unashamedly crying with the sheer emotion of the moment, tears running unchecked down our smiling faces. We were now "ATS," and within a week we ATS were posted to different units all over the country, some together and staying together for the next two to three years.

But most of us were shaped and guided for always by our training at Glen Parva Barracks. No, I did not get trained as a driver – some idiot of a drill sergeant reported my difficulty with telling left from right.

And, do you know – to this very day, I still don't drive!!

How I Survived the Wellie Trap

Let me set the scene for you. It is October 1960, and in the small market town of Watford, in Hertfordshire, England, lived a 32-year-old woman named Lyn Hatton. She lived with her feckless husband, Dick, and five children. Now, let me begin –

Autumn weather in England, to put it mildly, is changeable! But this particular October morning shone bright, clear, and crisp upon us – my visiting mother, myself, and my two-year-old daughter, "Young Lyn," who was cozily cocooned within her weather-proofed stroller.

We set off from home to trek one-and-half miles into Watford Town. Our target was the High Street, and, in particular, a rather "tony" shoe store named "Lilly and Skinners," where my Mum proposed to buy me a pair of much-needed winter shoes to replace my decidedly well-worn canvas sandals.

Halfway up the hill into town a sudden deluge of rain soaked Mum and me to the skin, but young Lyn stayed snug and dry inside the stroller. Eventually, we plodded soggily into town and headed for the chosen store. As I hinted before, this shop was *posh*. The entrance to it was set well back in a deep, V-shaped arcade. Vast plate glass windows showcased artistic displays of winter boots and shoes. Prettily positioned branches of artificial autumn leaves created an elegant background – all so very "ah-la."

Then we arrived upon the scene, a more-than-a-trifle bedraggled trio – that is, if you count the stroller from which rivulets of rain water continued to stream. We were not a very imposing picture.

The door at the rear of the arcade stood wide open allowing a view of the plushy showroom beyond, with its upholstered chairs and stools for the fitting of elegant shoes on elegant people's elegant feet. A tall, sandy-haired man wearing the obligatory – for those times – uniform of black jacket, white shirt, dark tie, and grey-striped trousers, was nervously watching us from within.

A satellite trio of black-clad lady assistants fluttered at the back of him. They were probably crossing their fingers in the hope we wouldn't squelch our way across the immaculate deep pile carpet upon which they stood. He, the manager, gazed in horror at these intruders coming into his neat, quiet, ordered world.

Now this was a man of forethought and an opportunist – that's probably why he was the manager – so when the rain storm started he had placed a row of tubs containing some very tasteful umbrellas halfway down the arcade. Also, this enterprising individual had arranged a long row of bright, shiny, new Wellington boots along the opposite side. We Londoners call them "Wellies." There was one boot of each size, from baby boots through great grand daddyWellies – black shiny, red shiny – all very shiny and new.

Guess who saw them first and wanted to try them on? Yes, I was tempted and went strolling down the arcade, leaving Mum with the baby. I found a lovely red Wellie in my size. I shucked off my soggy sandal and thrust my right foot deep into the boot. It was a trifle snug, but so-o-o pretty.

My mother scolded me for not waiting until I got inside the showroom, but they didn't add the word *impulsive* to my name for no good reason. But Mother was right. I'd better straighten up and fly right, and take off the boot! Um-m! – Er-r! – Oh, oh! – It won't come off! My foot is stuck. The equation of wet foot in tight Wellie equals – a problem!

Trying to force the Wellie off with my left foot resulted in the one remaining strap on my poor sandal to give up the struggle – and did not budge the boot. I leaned over the stroller and tried to stand on one leg and pull the boot off. I slipped, jarred the stroller, and frightened young Lyn who started crying loudly, which lovely sound became magnified as it echoed around the arcade.

Mother offered her arm, but the floor was now pretty wet and I slipped down, practically pulling her down as well. Desperation was setting in, so as I was sitting down there I asked Mum to pull from above whilst I braced myself against the plate glass window. She hauled on my leg with all her might, and I leaned back to aid her efforts. A loud creak from behind got my attention and, looking over my shoulder, I beheld the plate glass window bowing inward over its so tasteful display of shoes. At the same time a squeak from Mum drew my eyes to the front, where she now sat opposite me on the wet mosaic tile floor.

That is when I started to laugh! Then so did Mum. Young Lyn revved up the bellows from within the stroller – and so bedlam ensued. Still sitting on the damp arcade tiles we just could not stop laughing. We cried, laughing. We shrieked with laughter, with tears streaming down our faces, hiccupping as we tried to catch our breath.

Finally, still convulsing with laughter, we helped each other upright. Then I leaned back against the expensive plate glass window again! This was altogether too much for the shoe store manager and his staff, and, as the window once more bowed away from me, they rushed out of the door and bodily dragged me into the showroom. I was still chucking and snorting with hysterical laughter.

Mum followed us inside with the stroller and still-bellowing kid, but the laughter couldn't be stopped. Every time our eyes met, we exploded again.

Some time later, after the application of talcum powder amid many muttered threats from the manager, my foot was at last released from the "Wellie Trap."

It was suggested by "His Nibs," the manager, to my Mother – whom he had at last recognized as a real lady (if a rather damp one) – that she purchase the offending, and now ruined for sale, pair of red Wellies. Her reply, in true duchess style, was, "Well, *really* young man, I *might* – but they *very obviously* did not fit my daughter!" Whereupon she sailed, stroller before her, regally out of the store, followed by me, barefoot and still giggling as I left a trail of white talc footprints across the plushy carpet.

The Gathering

According to my well used and valued "Readers Digest" dictionary the word "Gathering" has many connotations: -- An Assembly, A Collection, To Muster, To Harvest, To Amass, To Embrace and so on. During our visit to England in May last year, 2005 Beris and I attended several "Gatherings" of the family variety and very enjoyable they were too.

But on the weekend that we spent at the lovely home of Ros and Alan Gill in the Lincolnshire Village of Nocton – we assembled, mustered, harvested, amassed and embraced to our hearts content.

Ros and Alan Gill were an important part of the life we lived for four long years in the Southern African Country of Botswana, near a native village named Palapye.

Expatriates – "Expats" – are a section of a gypsy group that chooses to take their work skills to countries and places that are off the beaten track – so to speak – in a word adventurers! In Palapye we lived in the Kalahari Desert, lot of beaten tracks, but only one macadam road that ran from Lobatse on the Southern Border to the Zambian and Zimbabwe Borders in the north.

We lived in an enclosed compound in newly built Bungalows and some of our early conditions were a bit primitive. Over the next 4 years things improved – but a degree of isolation was inevitable – we were the minority – white workers in a Sovereign Black Country. It was a fact and condition of our lives.

So our compatriates were our workmates, neighbours, playmates and friends if we were lucky – and we were lucky. Most of our people were great characters and life time friendships in sometimes difficult circumstances were formed.

Alan Gill was one of the top engineers on this big project – building a Hi-Tech Power Station in the desert next to a large coal mine. Alan worked on the set-up and erection of this giant "Meccano" Set – and he was a mechanical genius.

His wife Rosaleen (Ros) was a teacher and when younger expats with young families joined us she got permission to home school the children in her home, she started with 3 children at her dining table. So successful was she that after 4 1/2 years she was headmistress and administrator of a school teaching 180 pupils with 10 teachers, and 2/3rds of the children were from fee-paying Batswana families – she also was much admired.

Our leisure was spent in the pool that the Government had constructed for our use with a tennis court next to it. A tiny, garden type, shed near the pool was a paperback library by day and a well attended bar at night – these were our amenities. After a year of applications and an overall growth to over 80 people on staff and living in the compound we were finally given a club house with a hall, squash court and bar combined.

Four sets of "older" couples – "50-ish," became the group of friends that we spent many free hours with.

Swimming, tennis, all pursuits that from boredom became contests and so much planning went into the games and the weird prizes – but I remember the laughter the most. Alan, Derek, Beris and Geordie were always planning safaris and treks into the bush and up to the "Chobe" for braai's and campouts – some of which were very exciting.

So to bring this back to our subject – "Gathering" – can you imagine the mustering and embracing, the retelling and reminiscing – the jokes and capers that we assembled and harvested from our aging memories, collecting even more from this visit. Beris and I were greeted with true love at the door to their house and we started talking, staggered to bed at midnight then walked into the kitchen next morning for breakfast still talking and laughing.

A true meeting of minds – we spoke the same language, had the same experiences and loved the times we had back then.

Later we drove away looking like a couple of plushy inebriated Buddha's, -- soaked with words and sated with laughter.

We'd had a real worthwhile Gathering - Such a Joy!
AMEN

AFRICA

The Journey

My heart was sick, I did not want to go, this was no way to start another adventure but needs were very much the reason. My husband needed the work so we were going to Botswana.

The journey began at 5A.M. on a day in the middle of July 1986. An autumn day in South Africa, a cool clear crisp morning, to some, a good day to start an adventure.

We left from a hotel in Johannesburg, mainly because I willfully refused to stay overnight with family or friends. Parting from the beloved home and a accoutrements was a painful, heartburning experience and prolonged farewells were not my style. A hotel is a staging post, no need to hug and promise but just say thank you and off you go.

We travelled north through the Western Transvaal away from Johannesburg toward the far border, past Rustenburg and Mafikeng.

Zeerust was the last town before the border and the car, a hatch back V.W. Golf, was refueled and checked. The travelers needs were seen to also. 200 Klm's.had been journeyed so far and the day was getting warmer. As we went north, at about 8 A.M. the sleepy hamlets of North Eastern Transvaal were moving about their day, farms, mainly mealie/corn growers were all around.

With a silent prayer the journey continued, 200 Klm's. plus more to the border posts, habitation grows more sparse, more African villagers and workers on donkey carts, the animals daintily tripping along under the sometimes cruel whip and heavy loads.

Cultivated land almost imperceptibly becomes bush and scrubby trees, grey and tan, an all pervasive color scheme, almost as if the artist had run out of vivid shades on his palette.

We stop by the roadside surrounded by the scruffy bush, and drink coffee from a flask, sharing bitty remarks, no heart for the chatty stuff, then the little overloaded car goes tootling off along this long straight boring road again. But at least it has a good surface , and heat begins to send up it's shimmer before us and out of this eventually wavers up a sign post "Grens/Border Ahead".

The border post on the South African side is run by the immigration and customs division of the South African Police, backed by a trained platoon of border patrol personnel from the South African defence force. The office was in a neat brick bungalow type building.

The journey now rests at the border post, ultra polite smartly uniformed men and women check identities declaration forms e.t.c. and ask reasons for your visit to the country that lies across a few metres of land, and it is explained as briefly as possible, that circumstances have led to acceptance of a position helping to build a brand new Hi-Tech Power Station.

A small, wintry, smile creases the eyes of the Afrikaner Sergeant at the desk beyond the entry window and he said – "Best of Luck Mynheer en Mevrouw – go with God and come back home soon". It is now 10 A.M. and getting warmer.

In a continent so full of anomalies the relationship between R.S.A. is full of pitfalls for the know-it-all's who say they know what goes on. African States like S.W. Africa (Namibia) Angola, Botswana, Zambia and Zimbabwe call themselves "the front line states" stemming from the confrontation they had declared against the policy of Aparthied and the growing war readiness of the Republic of South Africa. They had become staging posts for terrorists and bandits which was vigorously and with much drama denied. Enough of that we must proceed.

Thro' a set of road crossing gates, over the bridge across the Limpopo River, then a few feet of *no mans land,* an earth road, that is patrolled continuously by South African armoured vehicles on border patrol up to another set of gates and into the "Republic of Botswana" and a true and immediate indoctrination into the world of a minority group – yourself.

The Immigration and Customs Dept of Botswana is run by the officers from in country. They work out of a window in the low white washed building beside a heavy barrier separated into exit and entry areas.

The line of people trying to enter Botswana seemed to consist of truckers carrying goods from South Africa, tourists on safari trips with licensed guides, natives returning home and newly employed persons about to take up a two year contract with the Government on temporary residence; we must all approach the window.

All paperwork, prepared beforehand, on advisement, is not enough to satisfy the immigration officer behind his window – no work permit had been deposited here by the Power Corporation and my husband is ordered to return to South Africa until the paperwork appears from the capital, Gaborone.

Time now being 11A.M. and the over packed car, parked in the sparse dappled shade of a scraggly tree on one side of the immigration area is very warm, and frustration and a new niggling feeling of – could it be – fear, creeps in.

A request to use a telephone is refused. My mate pleads with an adamant official asking him to call the company's Chairman, a prominent Botswana politician. After an hour or more a message was passed to say that the paperwork was on it's way from the capital, Gaborone, some 30 klms. distant.

I sat sipping warm Perrier water watching a customs man clip his toenails whilst sitting on a wooden bench outside the entry side office. After his pedicure he replaces his shoes and becomes interested in what I am drinking from the small green bottle. At his enquiry he is informed that it's just Perrier water and he saunters away.

Eventually the paper work arrived by messenger and we went through the item by item procedure to enter the Republic of Botswana. As the official completed his task he welcomed my husband to his country and I found out that I had become a dependent! What a blow for "Miss Lyn's" ego.

Our frustrations were tested anew after driving 26 klms. to find a military road block looming up ahead and once more we were signaled to pull over.

Our Transvaal license plates were to cause some further harassment on the journey. But these Botswana Defence Force Soldiers are polite and very smart in uniform and appearance. After scrutiny of documents and a further search of the car we moved onward to discover the delights of the Capital City Gaborone.

Soon to journey on.

THE MADAM'S MAN

Chink a Chink – Chink a Chink – Chink a Chink – the ring of something striking metal summoned me from the house out into the mid-morning heat. There, at the double gated entry to the front yard stood a youth of 16 or 17 years, tapping a stone on the top bar of the metal gate echoing an ethnic African drumbeat.

My sandaled feet crunched slowly across the newly graveled drive in front of the empty house, I was waiting for a removal van carrying our possessions to arrive so we could move into our new home here in Palapye, Botswana.

The fresh grey gravel was the only sign of order in this desert garden, it had more the appearance of an abandoned building site with empty paint cans and plastic cement bags vying for space with piles of broken roofing tiles and shards of splintered lumber. Lumps of knobbly concrete were pushing up through this dirty reddish sand, looking like weird growths of grey fungus.

Of course it was a building site, the house was newly built for us and the debris was the usual adornment left by most building workmen – just trash for someone else to clear up.

Skinny, almost to the point of emaciation, his brown skin dusty and grey looking, large liquid eyes shone out at me – seemingly hesitant to make direct eye contact – but he stopped beating a tattoo on my gate and dropped the stone into the dirt.

The boy had a large well shaped head and perched jauntily upon his wiry, crinkly black hair were the remnants of a once colorful red tartan Tam o' Shanter – complete with top knot bobble. Torn and dirty as the cap was he reached up and dragged it from his bobbing head, clutching it against his chest while breathlessly intoning his greeting – "DumelaMma—Dumela.

I returned his greeting and made the usual enquiries in Tswana – the local language - as to his state of health ? From where did he come ?and why to me ? In a nervous rush of words he informed me he had come from Serowe to Palapye on this day, and he added, " I must work for you N'KooKoo'--- startled, but amused I exclaimed, "you must ?"

To my amazement a flashing smile lit up his brown features. White, white teeth, large and perfect, embedded in purple gums seemed to use up half his face as he bobbed and weaved in transports of delight. Obviously he thought my sarcastic exclamation was agreement.

I studied him as we stood face to face across the gates in the hot African sunshine, whilst he tried in fractured sentences to tell me what a treasure I had hired.

He was about my height, clad in a clean but ragged shirt and pants, the legs of which looked as if they had been hacked off at mid calf by a blunt saw.

Large, very large, horny toed scarred bare feet scuffed and moved in the dirt as if to a distant drum beat. He was not the usual type of applicant for a gardener's job, but he was the first and also I was feeling at a low ebb just from being there. I had arrived a day before and was still unimpressed by my surroundings.

" What is your name?" I   asked. The shuffling stopped. The smile disappeared. "name is N'Twakolo – am call by Meshach – from Bible, Mma"

"So Meshach, what money?"

"Ten Pula, one day" he whispered. I smiled. Well, he could try couldn't he? " Meshach, you work good the madam she give four Pula, one day".

The huge smile attacked his face once more and the dance began again, "is good Madah, I come now!"

I had been in Africa long enough to know that his eagerness to start work mean't that he was hungry, so I sent him to the back of the house and said I would see if I had food. The very large feet carried the huge smile around the corner and I went into the house smiling to myself, maybe at myself a little as well.

African workers like plain food in large quantities and big tin mugs of very sweet tea –"Almost like taking a dash of tea with their sugar"

I made four large doorstep sandwiches of bread and cheese accompanied by the usual tea and took them to the back door. Meshach scrambled up from his position crouched against the wall in the shade. The cap grabbing , bobbing and weaving began again until I said," Eat now Meshach," and retreated inside so that he could be comfortable to eat.

When the furniture van drew up about an hour later my newly engaged and fed employee swiftly opened wide the gates and ran to push up the garage shutter door. The van crew soon allowed "The Madam's Man" to help them and his proprietorial manner implied that he had served many months as my aide. I did not deny him his boasting about my patronage, why spoil his day? – it had been a good one so far!

During the next four years Meshach helped me transform that desert garden on the Lotsane River bank , into a small Garden of Eden—well, It was to us!

He was a willing pupil , if a little slow at first – but that was probably because of our language difference. This was a young African who wanted to learn and did not mind what he did for us, even to helping me wash floors and hang out laundry when the housemaid failed to appear.

I taught him to lay paving and to speak English well and he took great delight in teaching me Tswana. I learned that "Madala" mean't wise older man, as in "Bricks Madala" (Beris was called "Bricks" by his men) and that "N'Kookoo" was "wise mother of my mother" – in rural African districts respect for the elders is paramount.

The most enjoyment Meshach derived was when Beris took him riding in the car. His, by now, famous grin would not leave his face for ages such was his delight, especially if his friends saw him riding – that was the cherry on the top.

Mr. Mololetsi, Meshach's father, appeared at my back door one day when Meshach was about twenty years old. He was a wizened weary man with bloodshot, sore eyes and scarred rope veined hands. He worked at the diamond mines at Arapa, in the Northern District, and his wife, Meshach's mother, kept his Kraal in Serowe and saw to the crops and children whilst he spent eleven months of the year at the mine barracks coming to his village for one month only at year's end.

We sat out back on the shaded deck and drank his choice of cool water. After about fifteen minutes or so of polite pleasantries, with his strangely subdued son translating a long harangue began the gist of which was that Meshach," had made a girl with child". The son's shame was the father's and the family's shame , and to top it all the girl refused the boy as a husband, - he was only a gardener.

The nub of the matter became clear when Mr. Mololetsi asked me to send Meshach's salary to his mother in Serowe every month. The parents of the young mother-to -be were demanding payment- for loss of lobola / bride price – and the Mololetsi family were honor bound to make restitution in full.

"But all of it?' I asked Mr. Mololetsi – he nodded his head, from which he had not removed a venerable dusty black fedora, I guess it represented his badge of authority.

"How will he live?" was my next query.

"By get more job. Go find more work," Mr. Mololetsi replied. "You his mother in Palapye not let go hungry".

So the matter was pursued and concluded and in due time Meshach became the very proud father of a beautiful baby girl.

I was given the signal honor of naming the child and I named her Lorraine, after a lovely brave girl I knew in South Africa, and the young father grinned with great pleasure at the layette and blankets we gave to him for the babe.

By July 1990 he had grown into a well developed twenty-one year old, a six footer with shiny brown skin and muscles. He even wore shoes and socks most of the time!.

By the time we left Botswana Meshach had become our trusted friend, house guard, my nursemaid, for a while pushing my wheelchair, beaming with pride. He could and would put his hand to any job about the place and he had learned many skills.

Of course, like most rural Africans, he took off now and again, to go "to the lands" to plant or harvest the sorghum crops or to the "cattle post" to brand the new calves, but he always came back after a week or two.

It wasn't all sweetness and light, we had some head to heads, mainly because of culture gaps on both sides, and he was a teenager—they seem to be universal somehow!

Beris, my husband, found Meshach a good job at the power station before we left Botswana and we hear through the expatriate grapevine that he still has it two and a half years later.

Meshach and his "Mada" both wept when we parted, but he had enriched our lives and I hoped we had bettered his.

LETTER TO AMERICA

Surely if you timed it that huge jaffa orange rising so fast out of an inky black sky would move every second.

The time is 5:00am. and another African day is dawning. The air is cool &moist, the dusky pre-dawn shadows hide the dirty, dry bush and scrubby trees. My attention is centered on this deep orange glow that spreads like dye poured into a container of clean water, it's gold tips everything it touches and for this moment there is nothing ugly in sight.

Last night we sat here in darkness under the Southern Cross and listened to the sound of drums over the bush, people so easily take up new religion and practice it in their yards in the bush or here in the low cost houses and go to consult a Sangoma midweek.

Suddenly a donkey tears the silence and reverie with his ugly bray. That seems to signal by echoes over the veldt that every cockerel in Africa must now begin to crow. It's so amusing to try and pick out the croaky learners, now a goat bleats, answered by his brothers and the chorus is so loud, what a row!

Whilst the sun has been rising an accompaniment of bush noises have gradually erupted into life. Pied crows are calling across the river and bird calls are sounding , close to me a bird is raucously warning off the cats in the garden.

It is such a lovely morning, with just a tiny breath of wind, all my flowers are in bloom and seem to be standing tall to be noticed – the Zinnias in so many different hues, Cosmo Daises, Star of David, the sky blue of the magnificent GrandifloraThunberga – pretty pink petals on the 'Mile a Minute' screen, pink geraniums, and the yellow and flame of the Cannas. An oasis in the desert – the Kalahari.

The sun is so bright now I must put up the sunshade or I will get burned. All the important things seem to get done very early Sunday morning here, many of the people will party or play drums most of the night sometimes , but then the hymns and chants come floating on the morning air.

I can hear chopping – someone is decimating one more of Botswana's dwindling trees to light the cook fire or perhaps they are a party of girls out to get roof poles for a Bride-to- Be , this will be her first step in a ritual.

The pied crows are always in evidence , but Sunday mornings are special for them. This early the company's laborers come with a truck and pick up the refuse. One man comes an hour early to put out the bins on the street ready for the truck. When he moves on the crows move in for a feast and their eating habits are quite medieval! Unwanted bits go over the shoulder.

There is a pied crow resting in a tree somewhere near and he is almost crooning, in a sort of growly purr, grrrr- toctotctoc (fast) – probably indigestion!

I wish I knew what all the bird calls were and to which species they belong, but my attention span wouldn't stay long enough for me to learn now that I am old.

The bush has grown and thickened enormously since the floods last year, we used to be able to see a village some 2-3 miles away and the single track railway line – Bulawayo to Johannesburg (a 2 day trip) – now it is 14 hours from Palapye to Johannesburg even today. So now the huts have disappeared in the new growth except for one or two still shiny aluminum cones that they top new thatches with nowadays.. Must be a bit dodgy in the electrical storms – I doubt they put in lightning rods ?

At about 5.30 am a train began making a great chuffing and hooting out there, so I got the binoculars and stood on the table to search for it. The morning was so still I could even hear voices out there , just speaking Tswana of course, but when I finally sighted the train it was a single little self important loco. – noisy devil - A touch of – I'm awake so must be you !

A herd of cattle are strolling past the back fence just now, going to graze along the river. They are looking good, fat and sleek, with hides shiny like amber satin or newly opened conkers.

There are two cowbells in the herd, different tones and quite mellow, they must have been in place around the beast's necks for some time. No herd boy.

The cowbells have faded now to be replaced by the noise of the dogs in the compound warning off the dustmen – you can tell the laborers progress by the different dog's barks.

Kathy's terrier ,Nibz, his yap means they are at the lower compound, sharp, high barks of Prebbles Kaffir dogs, shrill yaps of Smith's two Maltese – Mitzi and Brian, - James two dogs sound quite vicious and the Alsatians across the the road at Babs and Pete's raise the ante and volume . When the Lynch's Del starts in with his deep Labrador woof you know the men have reached the corner and heading out. I bet most folk are awake now !

Through all this our Sadie just lies and growls deep in her tum. "Been there – Dun that kids" !

The locals are amazed that we allow our dogs to bark; the dogs of the Tswana are debarked to allow them to be used in the hunt for food. They hunt with slingshots and air rifles to fill their cook pot, it is a very poor rural population.

Ah !the time must be getting on , I hear the sound of Tucker's Audi being revved up as they head off to church, only four of them now as the two boys went off to boarding school in England last week, they will be back at Easter I dare say.

I must move again- I feel the sun on my head.

The cats have finished their wild chases through the shrubbery, one is now suspended overhead in between the layers of shade cloth, it's Bella and she's talking to me for milk. "Macoaw" is her sound for milk, not got the pronunciation quite yet, but gets her requests across finally. "Tokkie" just bides her time and shares Bella's milk, Bella laps with her eyes shut tight – exctacy.

Beris has arisen and made tea and toast to eat out here. What a gem!

We have just watched a small local boy try and herd two scarred old donkeys down toward the village. At first he rode one but it kept stopping to graze and he got fed up with beating it with his fists and slid off to find a stick, they ride without tackle on the far rump of the animal. Anyway he soon broke his stick over the "Neddy's " back and even in Tswana that ten year old's language must have been blasphemous to the extreme. The anger and frustration in his shouts made us feel sorry for him.

Perhaps if we stop to analyze the situation thus:- this small boy has been sent out very early from his one blanket to get the donkeys – who wander miles- for his father to go visiting in his cart. Now that means get donkeys or get beaten .

So he spends two hours to find them and he left his hut still asleep so forgot the halters (if they have any) – no breakfast – no "cuppa tea" – just a hiding if he doesn't get 'em back.

No wonder they beat the heck out of those beasts when they grow up. A more recalcitrant animal I have to see.

Have been writing three hours - enough for one Sunday morning

Love Mum

PS. How would you pronounce the plural of Mongoose ?- Mongooses – Mongeeses Anyway they come at night to finish up the stray crumbs of dog/cat meals and leave little brittle "calling cards" on the deck for me to sweep up – hope their presence keep the snakes away.

SISTERS

In 1987 we had been living for one year just outside a village named Palapye in Botswana while my husband was employed at the Moropule Power Plant nearby. I had reluctantly and resentfully left South Africa, put a lovely home up for sale and my friend and helper Maggie Molefe was lost to me, I had no wish to mix into a new way of life and relationships. Such a spoiled brat!.

In those early days we were at times short on amenities and not least was the lack of medical services – the nearest hospital was in the capital Gaborone some hundreds of kilometers away, so we did the best we could in emergencies, as this story relates.The early morning sun gently touched my head and shoulders. Later it would be very hot. I sat, legs dangling, on the edge of a cracked decaying concrete loading dock. Alas! a frothing sparkling tide didn't surge before me, instead an expanse of dirty red Kalahari sand lay there dimpled by the myriad footsteps of donkeys, goats , cattle and humans – plus their trash.

My resting place fronted an ancient warehouse, once cream stuccoed, now scarred and moldered by time, it's dark, dank interior housed Palalpye's only vegetable market. At the furthest end of the wall behind me a door to a room stood open. The room with, whitewashed walls, measured about 6 feet wide and approximately 14 feet long with another door at the far end and was crammed with about 25 Batswana women of many ages and sizes – all waiting patiently.

This then was the waiting room of the "Women's Clinic" in Palapye, run by "Dr. Monica" who was a remarkable young person and not just because she was a black woman doctor from a third world country. Dr. Monica had style with a capital "S".

After graduating from Medical School she returned to Botswana and set up practice in Mahalapye, a town some 60 kilometers south of our village of Palapye. On Tuesday and Thursday she held this clinic, just for women in the end two rooms of this old warehouse.

Staffed by two nurses she had this space that was joined by a hallway which somehow housed the big cupboard dispensary run by the nurse/receptionist.

The Dr.'s office was a room at the very back of the building, it had a rudimentary bathroom and a curtained alcove containing a camp bed.

Everything was spotlessly clean, uniforms, linens, towels, utensils etc., the nurses were very calm and competent in their quiet efficiency. They ran the place with almost military precision.

Furniture in the waiting room comprised of a broken down settee that relaxed upon the floor, an easy chair in like condition and 6 or 7 kitchen chairs in varying stages of disrepair were in place around the pockmarked walls. Those women who had found seats were sharing , others leaned against the walls and door frame, some sat or squatted in native fashion upon the cracked and broken linoleum that had reneged on its job of covering the cement floor.

A couple of small children quietly amused themselves by drawing on the bare patches of cement using lumps of fallen plaster from the crumbling wall as chalk.

I was there because of an asthma attack that was degenerating into bronchus spasms making my knees twitch and coupled with the whistle my airway made as I tried to get air into my lungs, I was a sorry sight. Inquisitive faces were at all times popping out of the open door to investigate me and some even clicked tongues at my distress. My friend, Heather explained to the receiving nurse my problem and I scrawled my name on her forms.

So, there we were , all waiting.

A dusty , silver grey, low slung Mercedes drew up to the dock steps and our awaited "remarkable young person" alighted from it. She was a large boned, impressively fleshed woman, her stride was quick and confident. Theatrically dressed in colorful ,sweeping layered garments, she would not go unnoticed anywhere.

As the Dr. passed me going into the clinic, her dark intelligent eyes assessed me, acknowledging the presence of a very sick white woman on her doorstep. Something a trifle out of the ordinary for a Tuesday! She did not stop or break her stride and a rising murmur of greeting voices and hand claps accented her progress towards the days business in her cell like office where the nurses waited to place her patients before her.

Not long afterwards a nurse came out and with Heather's help moved me into the waiting room where two other patients gave up their hard won seat on the lowest part of the settee and I was deposited there like an honored guest. No one spoke, I couldn't, but moisture gathered in my eyes from gratitude. As you can guess I felt the gaze of many eyes as I shut my own and tried to ignore the trickle of tears running off my nose.

The nurse told my friend that Dr. Monica had insisted that I be brought inside. She had not appreciated the crowd of gawkers , children and dogs that had gathered near the dock to witness my unmusical performance. It was free entertainment for easily amused country folk.

More quickly than expected, I was lifted up and helped into the Dr's. room where I was charmed and relaxed by her manner, then quickly impressed with her diagnosis and swift emergency injection, after which I was lowered onto the snow white sheets on the camp bed , to rest, and the curtains were drawn.

Totally confident in her, I rested.

An hour or so passed as Dr. Monica carried on with her clinic, what did I know, since I spoke and understood only rudimentary Tswana my presence wasn't intrusive. When after a further examination and dispensing some pills the Dr. allowed me to go home saying she would call at my house on her way back to Mahalapye.

I asked Dr. Monica if her other patients had allowed me to go ahead of them and she said she had asked them if they would let me go first, they all agreed that I should and many of them still waited around to see if I was well.

As I left that poor waiting room with the plaster falling in chunks from the wall and the linoleum disintegrating on the floor I clasped my hands together and opened them in thanks many times towards those women in this poor African village in their humane action today that had made us sisters under the skin.

A week later as I returned to the clinic for a checkup, I was greeted and shaken by the hand and for a long while in the village , faces I could not remember would light up with a smile, a hand clap and knowing nods, I had many friends who remembered me.

The Bull

The four men were workmates and friends, one a native Motswana, the other three British expatriates. They had come together through their work commissioning a new hi-tech power station in the Kalahari desert, and were now enjoying a three-day safari together in the bush.

Batch Machangwani was of the Kalanga, a northern tribe, from whom came some exceptional people, whose strict moral codes did not stop them from educating their people to their utmost. Batch was with the party for his languages and ability as an animal tracker – about which "untested" skill his companions teased him continuously.

Alan was the testy "Geordi" from England's northern tribes, a hairy, bearded, gangling man of uncertain temper and proven mechanical brilliance. He was the leader of this small, fraternal expedition by virtue of the fact that he knew what he was doing.

Derek, a tall, handsome, silver-haired Welsh man, whose voice, musical to the lilt of his homeland valleys, was ever pleasing to the ear. He also was an engineer, but a complete novice in the bush. The first time they took him on a safari, he sat fishing on the banks of the River Chobe, surrounded by a family of warthogs, snuffling, squealing, and rooting around him – they were probably amazed by the sight and sound of Derek sitting there singing Welsh hymns to them. The story is told to this day, with embellishments, of course.

Beris, the fourth man, was a man of the Lincolnshire Fens, those lands overrun so often by the Danes, Vikings, and Norsemen of ancient British history. In jest, he is told he is the living example of a Danish rape and pillage raid, a rounded, square, sturdy frame, blue eyes, blond hair, and features and smile to win wars. Also a learner at this game and not an engineer, he is the company's supplies man, and happy to be there – just being.

The party was out three nights and had found nothing to hunt – someone must have put out a proclamation and the beasts had headed off to pastures new. A decision was made to return to base, and the party – transported in two Land Rovers, Alan owned one and Derek the other – set off on the single track across the desert toward the nearest large village of Serowe, about 30 miles distant.

It was late afternoon and very hot, about 104°. In the distance, like a mirage, wavered indeterminate shapes, leaping and shimmering in the waves of rising heat. The obstruction on the track ahead was finally defined as a beaten-up Toyota Land Cruiser hunkered down in their path.

It was surrounded by a crowd of scantily-clad, squeaking, clicking, chattering bushmen – women and children whose day had been made by this unexpected entertainment, they capered about in sheer excitement.

Three Africans in a semblance of European dress turned hopeful faces toward the small convoy of Land Rovers, now stopped on the track. They raised hands in supplication to the men now descending from the vehicles. The obvious leader of the stationary group met Batch as they approached.

Dust thrown up by their arrival settled on the heads and shoulders of the newcomers, not that it could have worsened their appearance much – unshaven, unwashed, uncombed, three days into the clothes they lived and slept in – in other words, a typical safari return.

But their own pungent odor was surpassed by that of the crowd that greeted them. A mass of Bushmen with the accompanying whiffs of cow dung, sweat, sour milk, all overlaid by an acrid whiff of the smoke from cook fires, that smell can get a European moving out on his way fast. But the irony is that these people think that we stink! They say they can smell the dead meat we eat. So much for all the mouthwash and deodorant ads.

After a rapid exchange of the polite amenities, handshakes all around, "Dumela Rah Dumela, How are you?" – the driver of the Toyota told the story of his "matata." It was obvious the vehicle was kaput, but the driver thought he saw salvation in the arrival of these white men in the desert.

The truck was so far down they could not see under it, and it was jerking spasmodically as if it were trying to revive itself. Imagine if you will, the expressions of the newcomers when they peered onto the back of the truck and gazed upon a huge, very angry, grey and white Brahma bull. He was so enmeshed in a web of rope he could only jerk and emit growls and low bellows, promising death and destruction to all the world about him.

The driver and his companions were taking the bull to Serowe for slaughter – it had taken three days to catch and load the unwilling passenger. The bull had to be transported live for the inspector to pronounce it wholesome.

The safari group had differing reactions, one got the video camera, and mechanics lifted the bonnet and examined the engine – the diagnosis eventually was that it had to be inspected from underneath and that could only be done by letting the bull go.

Oh, the wailing and gnashing of teeth! After some thirty minutes of arguing, only the decision of the safari group to continue on their journey made the driver agree to let the bull go. As he and his friends got out knives to begin to cut the ropes, a frenzy of activity began. Alan grabbed the video camera and climbed up to the roof of his Land Rover. Derek asked Batch to reverse his vehicle out of the way, and Beris climbed up with Alan. With Batch busy reversing his vehicle, Derek stood on the front fender of Alan's truck to get a better view of the game.

The unhappy cattlemen began to hack at the ropes securing the bull. They shouted and gestured to the Bushmen to get away, but on the whole they were ignored – fear overcome by the Bushmen's inquisitive nature.

The task of cutting the ropes began on one side and the tailgate end. As soon as that beast felt the ropes giving he renewed his struggles, causing his tormentors to dash back and forth slashing at ropes willy-nilly. Suddenly, with a roar and a heave he half rose up, ropes pinging and twanging apart around him. Another mighty heave and he turned the truck over on its side.

Just imagine a very annoyed, very large Brahma bull standing, trembling with rage and fear and exhaustion, festooned with scrappy lengths of rope, surveying the area of his release with revenge in his heart. Still tethered by a couple of ropes, he tried to move away and only succeeded in dragging the truck a few feet.

The driver, a man who must have been a fatalist at heart, crept around the truck and struck at one remaining tether, and the beast was loose.

Then the Bushmen moved, fast, pushing every which way, away from that bull. They ran for the Bushman camp, dived under thorn bushes and up stunted trees, and even under the two Land Rovers still stationary on the track.

As it lay defenseless on its side, the Toyota Land Cruiser was the first victim of the "John Bull's" attack mode. With stubby horns, it gouged great jagged scars in the metal work. On seeing this, Alan yelled to Beris to reverse his vehicle out of range, and Derek, perched on the bumper/fender, jumped off and ran toward his own truck shouting to Batch to "Ger it out of there!"

This movement caught the bull's attention and Derek became the new target. With a sideswipe at Alan's vehicle as he went by at a wobbly, fast lope he chose Derek, and they began a macabre "Round the Mulberry Bush" chase anticlockwise around the vehicle.

Every time Batch saw Derek run past the windscreen he swung open the left hand door, which Derek slammed shut in his terror to keep ahead of the bull. Round and round they went to the accompaniment of shouted orders from his companions – not very helpful until someone gave a long blast on a horn which made the bull pause to see where the noise came from, so giving a breathless Derek time to clamber to safety.

After a few charges and warning bellows "John Bull" decided to get the heck out of there, still stopping now and again in his retreat to look back and bellow his taunts at them.

They had willing hands to get the Toyota back upright, and further inspection proved the vehicle to be beyond repair. There was no oil in the rear differential, and the teeth had been ground off. The unlucky cattlemen were given a lift to Serowe.

The Bushmen's children got hands full of boiled sweets thrown to them and they fell over one another in the scramble for goodies, white teeth shining out of brown, dusty faces. Their tribe had a new story for the telling at the campfire through the years.

No video epic was born of this dramatic episode. The film consisted of swooping vistas of sky, sand, bush and hurtling bodies, but nothing to make sense of.

There was a film made in the 1980s about the Bushmen of Botswana titled *The Gods must be Crazy*. In retrospect, a thought suggests that if a film had been made of this, it could be titled *The Gods must be Laughing*.
Batch never did get his badge for tracking, but they were content.

Seeing is Believing – I Think!

As you rounded a bend going north "The Hill" erupted into view, towering from the flat bush-filled plain into the blazing blue sky. Espying it from far in the distance it seemed odd and out of place, almost as if it had surfaced overnight. But The Hill had been there for centuries, a natural citadel, a fortress against wild beasts in both human and animal form.

Our small coterie of expatriate friends gave it the name "iron-age hill" when we discussed it, fact and fiction combined to name the place and it was a source of speculation and curiosity and we all agreed that we must explore it – someday – one day.

Resting as it did on the sands of The Kalahari Desert, my imagination could visualize the hill crouched like a leopard or caracal, at rest, haunches raised up on folded rear legs, head laid on paws, watching, waiting.

The place seemed to draw me, and yet stories recounting it's antiquity and history sent nervous quivers skittering across my consciousness.

During my youth I had experienced some rather scary intuitive moments and had scoffed at them as coincidence. But now and again, over the span of years, 'things' happen, questions are raised but not fully explained. Maybe, just maybe something is there, suffice it to say I no longer scoff. On the day of my first, and only, visit to The Hill there definitely was "something there".

After months of procrastination the group at last agreed on a venture to The Hill, and a date was set in late October, early spring in Southern Africa.

A Sunday was the day set for the safari into the bush, Sunday was a day when work shifts allowed time off for most of the men. Two Land Rovers were made ready and provisioning began, we were a party of eight, four couples and our preparations were soon underway. Ice chests were packed with chicken, steak and "boerewors" – (spicy farmers sausages), bread-rolls, salads, fruit, vacuum flasks of coffee and ice packed wine and beer. Lots of water jugs and extra fuel for the vehicles. Folding chairs, iron grating and braai implements, plus cast iron cook pots, were included for this was a cook out day.

We set off in the cool of very early morning, 5:30 am, dressed in sweaters and tracksuits over tees and shorts, our thin tropical blood letting us feel the nippy dawn air. An atmosphere of light-hearted exhilaration and sense of adventure sparked among us. Speculation was rife, what might we find? Even – would we find anything? All were full of the good natured chaff and semi-insulting banter usual among the members of this group of friends.

So – we set off from Palapye heading north. Botswana had only one main metalled road and when you travel along it going north, up country from Palapye, for approx. 50 miles and then look to the left, you see it quite clearly – The Hill.

A block of soil, rock, indigenous bush and stunted thorn trees, it was almost in the shape of a gold ingot, wide at the base it rises about 600 feet into a plateau that is approx. the size of a soccer field. 1½ acres long and ½ acre wide.

When we reached a gate just off the highway that was thought to give access to the general area of The Hill we found an almost illegible hidden notice board, it had obviously been used for target practice by local marksmen.

The board was an official legend of the place and it gave us the name, it was named Toutswemogala Hill, and had been home to one of the largest villages in the country 1000 years before. The inhabitants had been a Bantu speaking people who were of a mixed tribal lineage and who evolved into the Tswana people of today. Botswana means "Place of the Tswana people".

Artifacts that had been found on Toutswemogala had been dated back to A.D.150, and showed the totem of some of the clans in this area, the crocodile. They were the Kwena People, Kwena being Tswana for crocodile.

Aware that we must ask permission to be in this area we set off along the rough track toward what we hoped would be a headman's village. The rough red sandy track we were jouncing and bouncing along twisted and turned through a amaze of thorn and mulberry bushes, finally opening out into an area of hard packed earth. Before us was a bush village, a typical conglomeration of mud walled thatched huts.

The village covered approx. 1 acre of land, and a form of defensive fence had been erected around the huts. A row of roughly axed slim tree trunks and thick branches were sunk into the ground and placed about a yard apart. These surrounded the native dwellings and the spaces between the posts were filled with close packed branches from thorn bushes, thus making a thick security wall against all invaders. At night the main entrance is blocked by the placing of more thorn bushes and believe me the African thorn bush with it's 5" and 6" white tipped thorns makes a very effective deterrent.

A single large thorn tree stood in a small courtyard before the largest hut, the Headman or Chief sat on a wooden chair in front of his house in the shade of the tree and motioned to our men to approach. Around the courtyard were walls of hand plastered mud, these would have been constructed, painted and decorated by the women of the village, as were all of the huts and the outer fence.

The courtyard is called a Lalwappa and some of the decorations on the walls included crude drawings of crocodiles which meant that these people are Kwena – "Crocodile Clan". A cleared space within the village also ringed by roughly piled thorn branches was the Kraal. At night the stock, sheep, goats, cattle and donkeys are driven into the encircling hedge to be kept safe overnight from predators, both "rustlers" and leopard or caracal.

The arrival of our vehicles caused quite a stir in the village. Children came running, many "Kaffir" dogs barked frenziedly and dust rose lazily in the early morning sunshine. Shy women peeped from hut doorways their hands over their mouths, laughing in surprise and embarrassment, but trying to be polite and not let us see them laughing at us.

Goats bleated in many varied tones and dashed all over the place adding to total uproar, and all the time the children were shouting –"Sweeties Mada, Sweeties", whilst cupping their left hands beneath their mouths.

We had some gifts with us, we knew that to present ourselves with respect, bearing gifts would go a long way to making us welcome. We had small bags of tea, salt and sugar, a pack of cigarettes and a mesh sack of small oranges for the children.

Permission to visit Toutswemogala had to come from the Chief, also directions on how to reach it.

I'm saying 'we', I should state that the men of the party did the negotiating and gift bearing. We women stayed out of it, remaining quietly in the vehicles. We knew that men who appeared unable to keep their women "in their place" would not have rated respect from the Chief and permission for our visit might have been refused.

Yes – even tho' the Headman had graciously accepted the gifts he could still turn us down.

You've heard of being 'stiffed' haven't you? Eventually the diplomatic overtures were all completed and a teenage youth was delegated by his Chief to guide us upon our way. With much arm waving and gesturing the tall skinny lad led us around the outer perimeter of the village. By this time we had lost sight of The Hill and as he led our caravan along a faint trail ??thro' the bush we began to wonder if he was trying to lose us. After about 15 minutes the trail petered out and so did our guide. He just waved us forward into what looked like impenetrable bush and loped off back to his village.

To say we were "slightly taken – aback" might tend to reinforce the legend of British understatement, shall I just say we were surprised! Be we were Brits and did have well pronounced upper lips—so - - - - we did the only thing we could do—we STIFFENED our upper lips— (collectively of course). And then we proceeded on (in the manner of Dr Livingstone and Sir Edmund Hillary— "onward ever onward" and 'because it was there") toward The Hill—where ever it was!

"Daredevil" Clyde Thompson drove the lead Land Rover and he just took off in a burst of automotive power, our driver, Alan Gill, not to be outdone sent his vehicle surging after Clyde. So began a very hairy-scary ride, up and over and even under bush and thorn trees, rocks and gullies. At one point we actually lost each other and only by calls, whistles and relentless horn tooting were we eventually reunited to plunge recklessly onward – towards our goal-we hoped!

At last – bumped, grazed and bruised, fingers cramped and aching from hanging on for dear life, we came upon a small clearing and there towering above us was The Hill.

We had made it! We would worry about getting out later.

The first order of events was to set up camp, unload chairs and cooking gear and make safe rock filled pits for our fires. But first and foremost the area was trampled and kicked by people in bush boots and thick socks to ensure that any unwelcome guests, such as snakes or scorpions, did not try to join our picnic. Gloved hands gathered wood and rocks for fires and holes were dug. Welcome cups of coffee were savoured whilst we discussed the scouting of a route up the side of The Hill.

For several days prior to this trip I had suffered a slight fever and sharp pain on the R.H. side of my ribs near the back, but I was the self-elected "chief woody" collecting and dragging back wood for the fires. I had been relentlessly schooled in the No.1 ritual for "woody's" and it was – "kick it – turn it over – then kick it again", just to make sure the wood was safe to pick up. As my efforts were <u>SO</u>important I soldiered on, "thro' fever and pain," not entirely uncomplaining, but doing my bit! I thereby gave the comedians a chance to air their friendly jokes and jibes at my expense.

So – enough coffee – enough talk, the men had scouted and found what looked like a possible path to ascend The Hill, so trouser cuffs were tucked into socks and the adventure continued.

The area from which we started to climb was a jumbled mess of large rocks and shale that had obviously fallen from above. Small, spindly bushes and shrubs had self set themselves all over and the going was rather risky.

Halfway up I stopped to catch my breath and ease my aching back, my friends, overtaking me, made teasing, derogatory remarks about geriatric's and hill climbing, then continued to climb in a laughing, scrambling colourful dotted line snaking up to the summit, leaving me to rest.

I relaxed and leaned back against the rock, pressing my ache into it, and gazed over the vista before and below me. There to the right the rooftops of the two Land Rovers and colourful splashes of the camp chairs could be glimpsed, thro' a sea of tree tops of thorn and mulberry.

The sky, a brassy blue in the mid-morning sun, was hard to gaze at and a slight chill breeze touched my hot dry skin, I stood there in a reverie of calm and rest.

The chill persisted and nearly became a shiver. A soft, almost imperceptible pressure upon my right shoulder made me turn my head that way slowly, still in my dreamy reverie.

There she stood an arms length away, hands clasped and cupped, elbows tucked into her sides in the universal gesture of supplication.

A bent, shriveled, very old African woman, one shoulder bared where her ragged draped blanket had slipped down revealing the grey wrinkled sac of a once milk filled breast. Her skin was dusty and her limbs were pipe stem thin and knobbly like the gnarled grey branches of the thorn trees.

The smile on her poor bony face revealed almost toothless purple gums, a few discoloured shards of molars were all she had left. Topping the skeletal frame of her emaciated body a plume of wiry greying frizzy hair nodded jauntily as she weaved up and down by my side.

"DumelaN'kookoo", I said in greeting – she did not reply, just kept on gesturing for alms.

"OotSooHeeli Jan – can I help you mma", I asked again. But the bobbing and weaving continued.

I felt in the pocket of my canvas trousers and my fingers found half a dozen paper wrapped sweeties. I offered them to the old black woman, her cupped hands extended to accept them and I dropped the sweets into them. At that moment Beris, my husband, called down from the summit, -- "honey where are you",? I turned my head and called up to him. "I'll just be a minute."

When I turned back to my old native woman she had gone - - - - -.

I supposed that Beris had frightened her with his loud shout, but she was no-where near where I could see, no-where to hide.

So I plodded on up, round rocks and bushes, slip sliding on shale until I crested The Hill top to be greeted with a derisory cheer and more banter about my advanced age - - - it's HELLbeing the eldest!!

From the top of Toutswemogala the view was impressive, mile upon mile of bush stretching into a blue haze in the far, far distance. Our party had split up and some searched for arrow heads and pre – iron age stone blade fragments. A few ostrich egg beads were found and identified as early Coinage. Photographs were taken and as the morning neared noon a few tummies started to rumble. We all agreed to return to camp, light the fires and get our meal.

As we gathered in a group to descend I asked, "did any of you give the old lady anything"? "old lady? – what old lady"? I was asked. "the one on the way up", I replied. In retrospect I must have been quite a butt for their good-natured jokes because they insisted that I must have craftily spiked my coffee with Brandy, or else I had a "handi hip gin" in my pocket.

There was no old woman on the path up – and despite my protestations – they were sure – so I shut up.

As we rounded the large rock on our way down, Alan said, "I see Lyn's been throwing her sweeties away". There on the path, in a little heap, lay six wrapped sweets! Without saying a word I scooped them up out of the dust and thrust them into my pocket.

We descended the rest of the way without mishap and had a wonderful Braai, Good Food, Great Company, Talk, Stories, Jokes and Relaxation.

When it came time to leave we cleaned the campsite, made sure fires were quite out and that all rubbish would go with us.

The devastated bush tracks we had caused by our arrival showed the bumpy, jolting way out. As we passed around the native village we threw sweeties out to the yelling, racing children.

I didn't have any. I left mine on a rock at the bottom of The Hill, an offering - - - just in case - - - - - -

Going Calling

The house nestled behind encircling white walls and a barred gate, in the shade of tall mature trees. Among them were five venerable gnarled oaks, for which the house is named.

Such a very English Name, "Five Oaks", for a house that sat just off the Main St. of a real African Village. Surrounded as it was by many grass roofed mud huts, above the tropic of Capricorn in Botswana.

It was 2 pm in the heat of the day and I was calling on Lindi Arbi who lived in this lovely cool rambling house with the white shutters and vine covered stoop.

My mode of travel along the 3 klms.to the village of Palapye had been in a rusty rickety old African bus practically held together by wire and rope. The fare was 5 Thebe and you called out when you wanted to get off, then the "conductor" would untie the rope holding the door on.

I had become used to riding this bus to Palapye but my fellow passengers considered me quite strange, luckily my sense of humour was such that a few smiling greetings in Tswana to my nearest neighbours usually got smiles and nods in return and a modicum of reserved acceptance.

On my arrival Lindi greeted me happily and we sat in comfy cushioned wicker chairs on the stoop, and her house girl, Nandi, brought us a tray of tea and biscuits for our refreshment. We talked, having a lovely afternoon sharing stories of our different lives and strolling thro' the grove of citrus trees at the rear of the house with the children playing around us.

Lindi is married to Faizal Arbi a successful business man in the Palapye area. Faizal is a Moslem, born in this country to a wealthy Indian family. He met Lindi, a South

African, when she taught school up country at the company village of Anglo-American Diamond Mines at Orapa.

He, Faizal, is a tall upright good looking fellow with a head of crisp dark waved hair and beard.   A charming amiable, forthright man. Lindi is small 5'3 or 4", fair-haired with an English Rose complexion, luminous grey eyes and the features that can be seen on a Victorian Cameo. She is lively, intelligent and a loving generous friend.

Seven years earlier they had gone to visit India on holiday together, whilst there they romantically decided to marry in India.

Both are about 30 years old and have 3 delightful children, a 6 yr. old son, Riaz and 2 daughters. Nidia 4 yrs and the new baby Tasheem.

When my husband came for me at 4:30 pm he could not enter this Muslim House without Lindi's husband being present as this is the custom, but I left laden with a woven basket full of fresh picked lemons and oranges.

Our friendship with Lindi and Faizal Arbi was a joy and great pleasure to both Beris and me. We spent many happy hours in their kitchen together talking and dining on the spicy Indian food that Lindi prepared.

But my first call upon Lindi at home lives in my memory still.

The Day I Was
The Centre of Attention

If you live in a Third World country, or any place far enough distanced from today's standard amenities of civilization, life gets a trifle complicated – sometimes.

It was April, 1988. Beris, my husband, and I had been living in Palapye, Botswana, in Central Southern Africa for twenty-one months, and felt we were becoming used to the life – so much so that we had decided to renew our two-year contract when this one ended in July that year.

A week before Easter, 1988, I contracted a nasty bout of bronchitis even the desert air did not help, and the fact that there were no medical facilities available to us expatriates also caused difficulties.

At the Moropule Power Station which Beris was helping to build, was a separate compound which housed thirty to forty Polish labourers. They were accompanied by their Political Kommisars who kept the men strictly segregated, but they had a doctor who cared for the men, a Polish Dr. Andrej.

When I became very sick, a petition was made at the highest level to the Kommisars to allow me to be examined by their Dr. Andrej, and finally they agreed. Beris drove me, wheezing like a grampus, to the compound and we met Dr. Andrej. After explanations and examinations, all hindered by the doctor's having very little English, and of course we had no Polish, he gave us medication and we left.

During that evening my condition became serious. I was almost comatose with severe vomiting and spasms. Dr. Andrej was allowed to visit our house on an emergency basis. And he and Beris deduced that the medication was Penicillin-based, to which I am allergic. Obviously the language barrier had nearly proved fatal. For two days the doctor visited and treated me continuously, and over the next week I recovered enough to venture out.

My first walk out was four houses down the road to visit my friend, Kathy. I sat and watched her use her sewing machine, and we were chatting when suddenly I collapsed.

From here on, my story is mainly hearsay. Kathy sent for Beris from work and he went for Dr. Andrej, who initially diagnosed a minor stroke (or C.V.A.). He suggested they take me to the native hospital in the village of Serowe forty miles away – "but *carefully.*"

They took me and I was in and out of a hazy sort of dream, but I do remember sitting in a wheelchair on the footpath outside his lab whilst a Swedish technician took blood. We were surrounded by a pushing, shoving crowd of Africans, an extremely interested audience. A very kind, but not very technical, African took my chest X-rays, leaving me still sitting in the chair. Finally, the advice of the African doctors was for Beris to take me to Johannesburg Hospital in the morning – if I survived the night. But how was he to accomplish this?

During the following night, fraught with fear and prayer, my poor, dear man held me tight, an at 8 a.m. next day we were in our appointed place at a bush airstrip some thirty miles away. Driven over by a good friend, Colin, in his Mazda 626 car, and accompanied by Kathy, we awaited the arrival of a single-engined Cessna plane which would ferry us to Johannesburg in South Africa, some 2 ½-3 hours flying time distant. There our daughter, Lesley, and her husband, Rory, would meet us with an ambulance.

Not really in this world at this time, I understand that the plane became overdue, to add to everyone's worry, but eventually at about 9:30 a.m. it arrived and I was bundled on board and laid on two seats, not an easy task in that confined space.

After a series of delays due to the disappearance of an immigration officer who was needed to stamp our passports to let us out of Botswana, all was ready.

But the plane would not start!!! The pilot, who was a power corporation employee, and his engineer were stumped. But the day got warmer and I can remember some of it.

After about two hours of attempting to start the Cessna, a group of concerned corporation employees seemed to have deserted the power station to help us at Serowe.

One bright spark suggested trying to jump-start the plane from the Mazda 626. A set of jump leads was borrowed from the manager of a government vehicle depot just up the road.

The horror stories about the risks the men took to make that plane start make my skin creep, but eventually there was a roar of noise, and it started. When it did, according to reports from witnesses, the spinning propeller was missing the right side of the Mazda's hood by about six inches. Needless to say, Colin inched his car to safety *very carefully*. I wonder if that was a first. What an advertisement for Mazda.

At midday, some native Africans were sent to herd the sheep and goats off the runway and we took off. We had to go up country to Selebe-Phikwe, to another tiny airstrip to get passports stamped, but I was not unloaded. Three plus hours later, we landed at Rand Airport at

Johannesburg, and after the usual immigration formalities an ambulance took me to Johannesburg Hospital for treatment – excellent treatment in a great hospital.

Some twelve days later I returned to Palapye after a six-hour car ride, partially paralyzed on my left side and with a regimen of exercises, etc., written out for me by the physiotherapists at the hospital.

But that is another story – suffice to say that from May I worked hard, and I visited Silverton, Oregon, at the end of August, 1988, travelling in a wheel chair and using a cane when necessary.

A lot of help, a lot of sweat, many, many tears and prayers, and also a smidgen of curses -- I'm no saint – went into my recovery. I will never forget the love and caring of my husband and all our compatriot friends in the foreign compound we called home for four long years.

Six Steps on How to Make A Garden From A Patch of African Desert

First   You find an African Male willing to help you, even tho' he knows that he's in charge.

Second   Access to plenty of water is a very great help.

Third   Fertiliser, plants, seeds, etc., must be transported hundreds of kilometres.

Fourth   A supply of unbreakable or bendable tools of a most basic nature is essential. Some gardeners could break or lose a ten-ton steamroller, given the opportunity.

Fifth   Many breakfasts lunches, and cool drinks must be provided for your helper, of course, because the average local diet does not consist of many items that contribute to strength or stamina.

Sixth   You need patience and an aptitude for learning native languages, both spoken and body, because you must explain your wants hourly, daily, weekly, monthly, yearly, and repeatedly.

But, eventually, you and your gardener will stand in the evening sun and gaze over what the Lord has helped you create and it is good.

The gardener's great, white smile tells you so.

Words

The conditions that bring forth hordes of frogs and toads to the banks of the Lotsane River at Palapye in Botswana arrive suddenly and startlingly. One moment the skies are clear and blue, and it seems that the next time you look, ochre and black clouds race toward you overhead, turning your day into the *dark* of night.

A blustery capricious *wind* comes bullying over the miles of scrubby bush, funneling up a dust cloud of dirty, red sand that seeps under doors and infinitesimal cracks in window frames, making a mockery of the hard work of my little maid, You can taste and feel the grittiness against your teeth.

The wind picks up and appropriates anything that is not either tied or weighted down. Soon another layer of trash will be gifted to the mucky environs of the village of Palapye.

Then the *rain* begins – so strong is the wind that from a window I watch torrential rain scythe sideways past the house. I have never before seen rain go *sideways* and am amazed. Such is the reaction of an urban-born person who is plunged willy-nilly into an almost *stone-age* rural life in the Kalahari.

Helplessly I observe floods of scummy, red-brown water rush in waves down the incline of our back garden heading for the river bank, taking my plants and soil along with them.

Two hours later the storm is past and we venture from our dusty interiors into the sunny, steaming gardens to assess the damage. Meshach brings the hose to wash down the dirt-splashed outer walls of the house. I wonder, do we need to add more water to the deluge? But he did think of it himself. Oh, I love that boy – he keeps me hopping, throwing me a curve ball like this now and then.

Phones start ringing in the compound. Damage reports and tall stories are related, and the day moves into evening.

Sitting on the paved deck at dusk, sipping our usual evening libations, we look out over the river to mile upon mile of bush that is covered with steamy, shadowy wisps of fog causing a slight unease. Was that a movement? Is something sliding past? Imagination can be a problem sometimes. There! Was that a phantom Zulu warrior sliding through the mist, cowhide shield raised and right hand grasping an assegai? Are there others out there – rising up in the mist to finish what they started a century before when they hunted the Tswana people like animals? The Tswana ran rather than be slaughtered, and this area was on the route of the brutal, warring tribes of Natal.

But what was that awful noise? A CRAAAKK, CRAAAKK, then another. A different tone joins the first, and soon the air is filled with a dark, pulsating rhythmic sound that lasts all night. It is the mating song of the African frogs and toads, answering a surge of hormones that call for a renewal of the species.

It is the first time we have heard this phenomenon that has been triggered by the rains, but by the time it has lasted two or three weeks the novelty has worn off, and we wish they would just – *shut up!*

The Treasure
Horison View
Johannesburg R.S.A. Nov. 1981

The early summer morning was gorgeous. All the windows and doors were open wide inviting fresh cool air and the sounds of birdsong to infiltrate the house

Shading the front entrance, a large slasto stone paved arbor enticed with a setting of garden chairs and table. Wisps of breeze moved branches overhead making a dancing dappled pattern of sun and shade upon the floor.

Multi – coloured petals drifted from the trellised roof where heavily scented jasmine rioted with dense cerise bougainvillea and creamy yellow roses.

The distinctive squeaky complaint of the gate at the end of the drive gave early warning of the arrival of a visitor. Steady, plodding, heel to toe footsteps advanced toward the house – and then – she was there, a large buxom woman, with coffee coloured skin that bloomed with a sateen sheen and very white teeth that showed a few gaps. Her lustrous black eyes saw everything until she became shy, coyly glancing down with a nervous smile and her hand rose to her mouth to hide the gappy teeth.

Standing four square in a pair of clumpy black oxfords she spoke – Good Mora Madam – Good Morning, I am Magdalina Molefe, to be your maid, I have my letters". Once she was seated in the shady arbor and refreshed with a glass of water she deposited a worn hand bag upon a spare chair and taking a handkerchief from a pocket of her cotton print dress she dabbed at beads of perspiration over her nose and upper lip.

Upon her head, seeming almost welded there, was the ubiquitous black beret, as is worn by 75% of suburban African women, almost a badge of her religious faith.

Tiny rivulets of sweat trickled from beneath the tight leather banded edge of her beret, no wonder she was hot, the walk from the tiny station took 10 mins. and was all up hill. Graciously she accepted the invitation to use the bathroom in the servant's quarters and returned looking much more comfortable.

Her quiet soft voice complimented a serious manner which was firm with no nonsense.

Magdalina Molefe knew who she was and what she was about. Terms of employment were quickly dealt with to our mutual satisfaction and Maggie, as she insisted on being called, plodded her dignified way back to the station and her home in the township of Tembisa.

During April 1986 Maggie helped nurse me after I had major surgery for cancer. Her caring for me and the time she spent with me as a friend are part of my memories of her.

Over the following six years she became my teacher and friend – it seems she took me over on the day she allowed me to become "Her Madam".

THE CALLING

Image of ferocity – Images of pain
Feelings of timelessness over barren dusty plain
A cruel land – a yoke of labour's essence
Man and beast strive each day in fear's shadowy presence
Rose gold dawns chase night time black away
Sun rides high in copious blue for yet another day
A child too soon born gasps and passes through
To fertilize the cycle as fragile as dew
Sparse on Mopani leaves open new.

Heat of noon a crushing weight
That slows the pace to sluggards' laborious gait
To droop and sleep in spurious shade
Need for rest eclipsing thoughts of being paid.

Evening shade's, purple and glorious orange-gold
Brings some release
And the beasts, rib gaunt with heads drooped low,
Pass slowly away to night's ease
The night sky is suddenly black velvety vastness
Southern Cross diamonds strewn across the softness.

The restless body twists, turns, soaks sheet and humble
pillow
Cruelty hides and death is o'er the farthest billow
It calls from far to mammon's distant shore
Calling deep in the heart, a skein of gold, of love –
For Africa once more.

Shades of the Importance of Being Earnest

Preface: The title of this piece needs to be explained "Shades of the Importance of Being   Earnest" is an allusion to the article of my deliverance. As in the play by Oscar Wilde.

The South African Airways flight from Johannesburg to London left Jan Smuts airport three times a week at 6:30 in the evening. The flight is long – very long, tedious and exhausting, with a good tail wind it could take twelve hours flying to Heathrow but if Europe was sending gusts of hot air our way the journey could take longer.

Beris and I were off on six weeks leave, we would spend ten days in the United Kingdom visiting relatives and friends and then proceed onward to Boise Idaho USA to stay with our daughter Joy, Son-in-Law Kelly and their family.

We were very tired. Beris from overwork and I recovering from dental surgery, with complications that left me desperately trying to cope with a new lower dental plate.

Surrounded by family and friends all there to give us a rousing send off, we were finally forced to stop partying and board the 747 and settle down. That was accomplished only to have an announcement broadcast to the effect that an electrical fault had to be fixed – sorry – eee!

Luckily Beris had booked our seats at the very front row by the exit door and of course the toilets. There is much more leg room and people stretching their legs in flight tend to talk to you, short stilted conversations – but at least contact. In the row behind us sat two American ladies, teachers going on leave to up-state New York from a school in Swaziland. I got the impression that they were missionary's, but they didn't say so directly.

Two and a half hours late the plane finally took off and we began settling into the encapsulated world of a long haul aircraft, trying to hear all of the captain's messages and watching a very pretty, extremely bored stewardess mime, to a recorded voice over the speaker system on how to inflate the life jacket, blow the whistle, (and use the brown paper bag—Joke!)

Dinner is served, in flight film, then lights out.

I never sleep on planes but the steady drone of the engines sends Beris off – no problem. I watched him for a while relaxed and bubbling and I decided as it was now 1:30 am I would try to sleep. So I curled my legs up and snuggled into the totally inadequate airline pillow and cellular blanket determined to try.

The pain in my legs was awful, I must be paralyzed, where was I , who was I ? Thrum, thrum, thrum went the engines, realisation dawned, I was back once more in the cabin of a 747 chugging through the night toward Europe.

The terrible cramp that had awoken me got worse – then eased as I made myself move. Bleary eyed I looked at my watch – tilting it toward the side light, 4:30 am – wow. I had gone to sleep, glancing at Beris happily blowing bubbles I went to the bathroom, I always overdo mineral water on long flights.

Splashing water over my face, then dabbing at it with a paper towel I saw in the mirror that some thing was out of place – but what? Oh my lord, my teeth – the denture was gone, what a cliffhanger.

I frantically felt in my pockets, No! Quickly exiting the claustrophobic atmosphere of the tiny bathroom I stepped to my seat, carefully lifting the pillow I felt under it, No! Slowly, almost tenderly gathering up the blanket I gently shook it. No pink and white piece of delicately sculpted plastic fell to my feet.

Panic rose up in me, hold on – I commanded – keep calm – no one need know, on hands and knees I swept my hands over my seat and down the sides – the floor – the springs. Then kneeling there I began to cry, the prospect of six weeks on holiday – no teeth – no smiling – butt of every stupid joke, laughing relatives could think up – and – I still had to tell Beris.

Lights slowly came on and a quiet voice over the intercom told us that we were over the Alps and would be landing at London Airport at 8:30 am GMT, only 1 hour late, and it was now 5:30 am.

Beris stirred smiled, saw my tears and sat up – not smiling. "whats up?" – sob -- sob – "hunny what's up": Sniffling and lisping – I whispered "I the loshed ma teef"! "you what"? "I – the losh ma teef"! Pointing at my lower jaw"

"Bloody Nora" exclaimed my doting spouse, "find em quick" –" I – looked" – "well look again" exasperation in every tone, he left to go to the bathroom distancing himself from me – my carelessness, my tears and probably to say a fervent prayer.

Still kneeling I began another fruitless search, a voice above my head asked "have you lost something my dear"?

I lifted my tired tear streaked snotty nosed face and met the gaze of one of the American lady teachers. Unable to restrain myself I cried "I – the losh ma teef" – Oh!

Your denture" she exclaimed – "oh my dear borrow this flashlight it might help". She handed me a nice little ladies flashlight, and smilingly passed me a tissue. Still smiling she left to join the line for the bathroom with her large Gladstone type leather handbag over her arm. Probably big enough to hold all her travel kit. I remember thinking – what a practical idea.

I used the useful flashlight to renew the search for the missing denture but to no avail.

I knelt once more before my seat, on the brink of another bout of blubbering when someone touched me on the shoulder – it was my kindly teacher – in her hand she held a wad of tissues, leaning down toward me she said – "is this what you've lost'? and pushed the tissues toward me.

Nestled in a bed of white paper sat my denture! I took the thing from her stammering and lisping my gratitude – "where did you find it?" I ask?

"It had fallen into my purse" she replied "under your seat." I returned my saviours flashlight and she move back to the seat behind me.

Clutching the wad of tissues that contained my delinquent teeth, I grabbed my toilet bag and sped to the bathroom, sharing a gummy but brilliant smile with all the people around me.

My vacation and my marriage had been saved by "A HANDBAG"!

OREGON

The Place

A joking remark is what started the ball rolling and from there we are here! in place on "The Place."

During our visit to Oregon from Botswana, during September into early October 1988, my husband, Beris, and I had a chance meeting with a local realtor. Terry Caster was showing our daughter and son-in-law some business property, and we went along just to be nosey. At least I admit I did!

Terry was very interested that we lived in Africa and jokingly asked if he could show us any property to keep us here. I, not to be out-done, immediately asked what property did he have to offer in Sublimity, as I admired the name and it looked like a nice little town. Laughing, the realtor said, "no he had not," and continued with his business with Joy and Kelly. Beris and I stood in the early fall sunshine and talked of our return to Africa in seven days' time.

Terry completed his business with Joy and came up to us and said, "I think I have something just for you, released from probate two days ago and newly listed." He looked straight at me and asked, "Do you want to go see it?" I must be glass-plated, or else he is a witch – like me! Sooo, "yes, please," I replied, "can we go now?"

My dazed husband was pushed into the realtor's car; Joy and I followed in her vehicle.

We travelled, in convoy, out of Silverton toward Silver Falls, then turned left and began to climb. We went up and up a twisting road that snaked ever higher through a long tunnel of overhanging trees, around a dangerous blind corner. And suddenly, there we were jolting along an unkempt drive toward the front of a very old, extremely

110

dilapidated, wooden house that had a three-step porch clinging for grim death to the front wall. Poor little house – many years before, the paint on the walls must have been a pretty yellow – alas not any more.

The house stood on eight and one-half acres of scotch broom – well, it certainly seemed to be prevalent – most of the high ground showed a liberal growth. Towering over the rear of the house stood five black walnut trees, the largest of which, by its girth alone, must have been the progenitor of the other four "volunteers." They cast attractive, sun-filtered shade over the grasses beneath their branches.

Apart from the level paddock upon which the sad little house stood, the rest of the land rose gently to a hill that flattened out to another paddock at the top. Up there, knee deep in grasses and weeds, grew a grove of 25 or so cherry trees backed by some large conifers. As we climbed the hill toward a derelict barn we disturbed a pair of browsing deer who flicked white tails and bounded off out of this obvious sanctuary.

Clearly the property abounded with deer. They made deep resting nests in the abundant scotch broom, and the heavy rank odor that permeated the area was a good indication as well.

I stood atop the hill in front of the cherry trees and declared, "This is where we will put our house," pointing to the spot. Don't think I didn't see the startled looks that the others exchanged, but, as is my wont, I chose to ignore them. It sometimes pays dividends to appear dumb.

Dilapidated as the outside of the house looked, the inside was even worse. The deceased owner had been an elderly bachelor, a smoker who lived in some disarray. But despite my initial feelings of utter disgust and dismay, my daughter assured me that "The Place" could be rescued.

My son-in-law, Kelly, suggested that a few firm nudges with a bulldozer blade might be appropriate, and I must admit that at the time I agreed with him.

Poor Beris! He didn't stand a chance! Kelly said the land was a good investment, Joy wanted us nearby and out of Africa!

I, well I fell in love. After standing on the rough gravel driveway looking all around I said, "I want it – I know it is for us." My broomstick was twitching!!

Twenty-four hours later we put in an offer for "The Place," and early on the day before we left to return to Africa our offer was accepted. A great deal of legal scrambling ensued. We opened a bank account, gave Joy power of attorney, and then set off on a three-day journey back to Botswana, the Kalahari, and another two-year work contract.

We immediately began realising our assets in South Africa, sold our house there, and sent all the proceeds to Joy, who did all the work in Silverton and Salem. By the beginning of November '88, "The Place" was ours. Joy sent to us the many pictures she took, and I sat in the Kalahari heat and pasted the best onto a sheet of cardboard. This was displayed in our house in Palapye, where for two long years we dreamed of cool, green grass and dripping trees, of daffodils in spring and cherry blossoms – even, as a long shot – scotch broom!

No one of our acquaintance in the compound at Palapye escaped being bombarded with pictures and stories about "The Place." They were kind folks who thought we were brave and adventurous, even if "over the hill." Thro' them we came to adopt the name we gave "The Place,"

born, I think, from repetition on my part, i.e., "Hi, Jimmy –
John – Joe, have I shown you these new pictures of 'The
Place' in Oregon?"

Our Joy worked hard, employed some teenagers on
clean-up and painting crews, but did much of the work
herself making the interior of the house habitable. She and
Kelly tore up the floor in one room and re-laid new boards
for the inimitable termites to chew on. New carpets were
put in and then the house was rented for a year.

Eventually, July 30th, 1990, came round and we
flew here to a house made clean and ready for us, food in
the fridge, flowers on the table, and the bed made up.

At last we were home – free and clear and paid for.
Thanks to the unstinting love and hard work of our kids,
Joy and Kelly – also to a lot of hard work, scrimping and
saving by us in Africa.

We love Silverton, Oregon, U.S.A., but we care
deeply for "The Place" that is our own, our home. During
the next few months a brand new manufactured house will
go up on the spot I indicated to them six years ago – and
then we will have come full circle. Halfway around the
world to "The Place" we love, we can't say better than to
repeat the old saying: "Home is where the heart is." Our
hearts are well and truly anchored here – so is my
broomstick!!

Home at Last

The kitchen floor jerked spasmodically beneath my feet – my brain shrieked "earthquake" – but no - the movement was rhythmic – it was the men working under the house in unison to jack up the floors, they had forgotten to warn me!

I sat, towel over my head, in a cloud of the dust of ages as the little wooden house creaked and groaned, the agony of being forced back to a normal horizontal position issuing forth from every joist.

Neighbours and friends had banded together to rid our home of the termites and dry rot that had infested the underneath of this 80 + year old house.

Beris, my husband, and I were over whelmed by the love and caring of these Oregonians toward a pair of older English immigrants to their country.

We were late in coming to America, but after a Gipsy Life in Southern Africa, we had bought land and come to live near our daughter, an American Citizen, and her family.

It was in late Aug. 1988 that we first visited Silverton in the Willamette Valley, Oregon. We fell in love with it's charm and scenery, and not least the warm friendly people.

We rented an R.V. and set off on a 12 day trip along the Oregon Coast and over the Cascades to Sisters and met many Oregonians. All without exception were well mannered and so interested in us.

First our English accents and then when we said that we lived in Southern Africa caught the attention of folks that we met and piqued their interest. Mostly we were asked if we were Missionaries, but after we explained that we were helping to erect a Power Plant in the Kalahari Desert our conversations almost became seminars.

On one Sunday in a restaurant outside the town of Florence our lunch time stretched to 3 hours whilst we had long conversations with other patrons, both locals and visitors.

In a store in Sisters even the customers lining up behind us at the cash desk joined in with the clerk to quiz us and we received many helpful updates about snow conditions on the passes in the mountains that day.

Many warm and genuine good wishes from the folks for a safe journey home to Africa, it seemed we knew no strangers.

A chance meeting with a realtor after our return to Silverton was to become the pivotal point that once more changed our direction in life.

We saw our 8 acres of land 5 days before our leave ended, made an offer on it which was accepted on the day before we were due to fly out on our long journey back to Botswana in Africa.

After empowering our daughter to purchase it for us we left. During two more hard slogging years in Botswana we realised all our assets and in July 1990 moved into our little house up in the hills outside Silverton. Paid for free and clear.

We are so lucky, the warm abiding friendship of our neighbours in this small community has lightened our lives and made us welcome.

We now know there are 50 United States and then there is Oregon and Oregonians and we praise the Lord for them all. They are a Blessing.

Who Needs to be a Hero Anyway?

The scream ripped through the peaceful morning calm. Kneeling as we were, comfortably weeding the flower beds, the piercing intrusion into this cosy domestic scene set our skins prickling.

Almost with primeval force the scream came again – and yet again – "Help me! Oh, Help me! Help me!..." The tones were strangled, the words almost incoherent. But nevertheless, our sorely tried nerves were all a-jangle and our skins tight with goose-bumps.

By this time we were on our feet, riven to the spot, our tools gripped in nervously flexing fingers, heads turning about looking for danger, eyes wide, fear etched upon our features. Almost palpably, the screeching had obliterated the peaceful sounds that had accompanied our quiet rural chores – the cosy clucking of the hens, crows squabbling in the tops of the pines, the whooping of the hummingbirds that had buzzed us attempting to chase us away from their nest in the quince tree, our murmured snippets of conversation – all here on this sunny, warm Saturday morning in this little valley so peaceful until a few moments ago.

We seemed frozen in place but by a great effort of will my husband moved, then so did I. He moved toward the road to rescue whoever needed it, me toward the house and safety – *My safety!* Only a few moments had elapsed since the screams had first assaulted our ears, but it seemed like an age. As we moved toward the drive, we agreed that it, the screaming, had appeared to come from uphill. *Now* the adrenalin was pumping. What to do? Should I overcome my natural inclination to cowardice and go with Beris, perhaps to help him overcome some awful assailant – *or* – better still, *hide!* Who was this panicky person? Get out there and stand by your man! We were newcomers here, we didn't know our neighbours well, and being "mind your own business" English, we hated to intrude. So we set off alone, together!

We had reached the gate by the road, and there I was, all unknowingly brave, clutching a handful of my husband's shirt. He showed me later the marks where I had grabbed flesh as well, but we were so hyped up he didn't feel it right then, and I don't remember getting to the gate at all. We turned right out of the gate, looking fearfully uphill. What awful sight, blood soaked body, or raging maniac intent on bloody revenge would we see? Nothing! There was no scene of diabolical ravaging – only a quiet, peacefully grey country road undulating up the hill.

"Go ring Jim and Penny," Beris said, "ask if they are all right." I began to argue – after all, even in an emergency why should I step out of character! But when he insisted, I jogged back to the house, casting many fearful glances over my shoulder to see how he was doing. I threw my gardening gloves onto the little front porch, wrenched open the front door, and rushed to the telephone. Oh Lord, there it was again, that terrible scream! My fingers were all thumbs, my brain a whirl. I could not find the piece of paper with their number on, for goodness sake it's not here! Look in the telephone book. Good idea – what is their surname? Oh God, I can't remember. What if Jim is fighting off a mad axeman whilst Penny is lying bleeding on the floor – and here I am dithering.

I spied Beris through the window. He was walking uphill. I ran out to the porch, cupping my hands to my mouth, I shouted, "Beris – what is their name?" "What?" he yelled back at me. Let's face it. He had a valid reason to be a trifle tetchy! There he was, an ordinary man, going into the unknown – and there was this harpy bellowing stupid questions at him over the fields.

Nevertheless I repeated my bellow, and, as Beris had by then reached their mailbox, he shouted back, "Derr!" By great good fortune, I forbore from asking him to spell it! I think that would have been pushing my luck a bit. Once more I ran to the telephone book and frantically search for the name, all the time aware that my dearest man is advancing toward an unknown enemy. Finally I scribbled down the number, lifted the receiver, and dialed. Please, Lord, don't let there be an answering machine – let them be all right.

The receiver on the other end is lifted, and the calm, measured, western country accents of Jim's voice sounded on the line, "Derr residence." "Jim, it's Lyn from over the road." "Well, howdy, Lyn," he said, "how're ya doin'?" My fear and panic gushed out over the line. I told of the awful screams and Beris going alone to investigate – and "Oh gawd, what should I do?"

So immersed was I in this dramatic story that at first I did not realize that Jim was chuckling. Had the man gone off his rocker? Was he mad?? He began to laugh really heartily now. "So, what's going on?" I yelled. "Oh, Lyn, I'm sorry," he replied, all the while coughing and spluttering. "Have you never heard Biggses' peacocks before? Our neighbors up the hill, the Biggs family, breed peacocks. Boy, it must be near breeding season for them to start that!" "Start what?" I said in tones of utter frustration. "why, screaming," replied Jim, and began laughing again. He finally pulled himself together and asked, "Should I call

Beris back down the hill and explain it all to him?" I said, "Yes, please," and replaced the telephone receiver with fingers numb from the white-knuckled grip I had upon it. My legs felt heavy, as if the strength had been drained out of them, and I collapsed in a limp lump onto the settee. *Biggses' peacocks!* What a cruel joke.

But – there is a coda to this story – and it goes thus –

Early one morning in February two years ago, a very cold morn, so frosty the blades of grass were standing to attention coated with hoarfrost, I was puttering about in my dressing gown getting breakfast. Beris was up at the tool shed feeding my rabbit and the hens. The phone rang. It was for Beris, and so I stepped through the front door to the little three-step porch and called him. No reply. Get out there and yell a bit louder, I rebuked myself it's not *that* cold.

As my slippered feet stepped onto the top wooden stair, the devils of chance, bad luck, and stupidity combined to give me a flying lesson. Up went my feet, down upon the edge of the second step came my rear end and my left wrist. *I bounced!* Oh, yes I did!! I bounced off of the steps onto the paved path below.

Whump!! all the breath I had inhaled to call my husband with was knocked out of me with a loud, groaning, *whoosh* sound. I lay where I had fallen, unable to move, numb and shocked. As my senses returned, I started feebly to call Beris to help me. "Help me, Beris, help me!"

Help came, but not what I wanted. It was Finn, our nine-month-old Blue Heeler pup who heard my cries, and she came galloping around the corner of the house. Not – alas – to the rescue. She thought I wanted to play. What other reason could I have for lying there if I didn't want to play? She licked me and pawed me while I tried to fend her off. She started to bark with excitement and kept on barking. And then Beris, fearful that she had dared to challenge a skunk, slowly peered very cautiously around the corner of the house.

What a sight met his eyes – his wife lay in a crumpled heap on the concrete path trying to fight off a large, very excited puppy. He came quickly to pick me up and was greeted by wails of, "Why didn't you come when I called?" To my dying day I will remember his reply. "But Honey, I thought it was just Biggses' peacocks screeching."

P.S. Beris left twice more for prolonged stays in England, and on wild stormy nights, you know, the mass murderer escapes and heads your way. I sat alone in the rickety old house, and I wondered if after the awful fate befell me they would engrave on my tombstone, "Sorry! we thought it was Biggses' Peacocks!!"

Preface

"Laughter is the Sun
That drives winter from
the human face."

Victor Hugo

When my friend Genie laughs heartily, she is a joy to behold. She has an irresistible sense of the ridiculous and her laughter has been my best accolade on several occasions. I write stories and one in particular so tickled Genie that I dedicated it to her and gave her a copy of this, "The Red Snapper".

RED SNAPPER

It was a lovely morning in early summer, 1992, in rural Oregon just outside the little town of Silverton. Beris, my husband, was still overseas and our good friend and neighbor, Jim Derr, had been over on his trusty riding mower to cut our large lawn. Jim does a great job, but the edges around the house still needed attention.

Now in our small wooden tool shed under the sheltering walnut trees are a few garden tools including a new motor WEED WHACKER and an old SNAPPER self-propelled motor mower. I stood in the doorway of the shed and surveyed the two items. Some of my husband's last words before he left were, "Promise me you won't try to use the WEED WHACKER." I promised – but he had not mentioned the mower, had he?

Well, out came that venerable machine with much grunting and tugging on my part – I'll swear it was grunting and tugging back 'cuz it was so awkward to move. Finally we were out under sunny skies and I cautiously circled the machine wondering what I should do first. Ah! check the fuel. I found a length of doweling and pushed it into the hole that had a cap named *Gas*. Well, it certainly needed some gas. So I got the small red can labeled *Gas* and sloshed a few deep guzzles in, recapped it, and shook the machine about a bit to wake up the parts and spread the fuel to wherever it was needed. These details will give you some idea of my mechanical expertise. Right – now you pull that string thing with the toggle on – but first push the switch to *Start* – nothing happens, except perhaps a strained right arm. What's that – a label – must get my spectacles to read it. Label says, "Do not put foot under here while starting motor." I remove sandaled foot from "under here" and commence to seriously start this machine which is rapidly building itself a character.

What now! The string comes up – and stays up! No juggling or wiggling of it makes it return to the depths of this pesky piece of junk. Someone has to go – so I leave and make a nice cup of tea and drink it sitting under the apple tree while the machine stands outside the shed and watches *ME*.

Revived by caffeine I returned to my adversary – this now has become very personal. Switch on – place foot in the correct position – and ***pull***. A cough! another pull – another cough. After several pull and cough attempts we get a roar of noise. I push a lever labeled *Throttle* – a louder roar issues forth. Boy, oh boy, I've beaten that beggar – it is now working, so I grasp the handle.

About here I think I should mention that the tool shed stands at the top of an incline, a little hill, and that near the back of the house, to the right, is a grassy bank with a gradient of about three in one, with some concrete steps a few yards farther on to the left.

My snorting, snarling, over-revving monster awaits my command. I squeeze the lever marked *Brake* and take off running – down the slope. Turn! ***Turn!*** Before the concrete – ***turn right!***

When that RED SNAPPER hit that slope, at what seemed like 40 miles an hour, my feet and lower torso snapped off the ground like a sheet waving on a wash line in a stiff breeze.

But I'm a doer – I hung on for grim death, rounded the far corner of the house and ran full pelt into a patch of the tallest, thickest, most luscious couch grass you've ever seen, and that old RED SNAPPER stopped dead and ended up with me draped, thoroughly winded, over the handle bar.

After getting my breath back, I tried to start it again – but it refused – adamantly – so in disgust I left it out there for two days whilst I sulked. Then I dragged it back up the hill and garaged it once more.

Two months later my brother-in-law visited from England and, despite my warnings of dire hardship, he approached the SNAPPER, and that fiend of a machine started *first* time and did a great job for him.

I can't help but think that the RED SNAPPER is a male and a misogynist to boot!

The Gift

In our little house up in the hills outside Silverton, I was preparing to visit Anna Beauchamp, my neighbour and friend. It was a Sunday afternoon in April. Beris had returned to England two months earlier, and I was bodging along until he returned.

As I was about to leave, a knock sounded at the door. I opened it, and there stood Pam Derr and her daughter, Tricia. Upon my invitation to come in, they both about-faced and retrieved some items from behind them on the porch. Advancing inside, Pam deposited in the centre of the room a large, white polystyrene box that was covered with a towel. Tricia placed a plastic pail with a bright blue lid beside the box.

"What have you got there?" I ask, whereupon Pam whipped the towel off the box, like an exuberant Italian waiter hoping for a big tip, and revealed six yellow, speckled chicks. My eyes must have bugged out like chapel hat pegs, because my visitors both burst into laughter and commenced to explain that the chicks were a gift – for me!

All my family will vouch for the fact that Mother is rarely rendered speechless. Too bad that they were not there to witness the phenomenon.

After some chatter and more laughter, Pam and Tricia left. I would follow after I had settled my new pets. As a means of securing the chicks, I placed a piece of plywood weighted down by Volume L to Z of the *Reader's Digest Illustrated Dictionary* over the top of the box. I was still in shock!

On returning from my visiting, determined to decide on a course of action, I was greeted by the spectacle of our three cats, Tokkie, Missie, and Bella, arranged in a semicircle around the white box. They were obviously intrigued by the cheeping coming from inside. On greedy Bella's face was a look that said, "May I see the menu, please."

Finally I decided to lodge the chicks in the attic temporarily. Tomorrow I would deal with the problem. So I put the box in the attic, fixed up a spare bedside lamp for warmth, replenished the water, took some chick meal from the blue-lidded bucket, and then went to bed.

Monday dawned and my daughter, Joy, phoned whilst I was upstairs gazing at my new charges. She asked why I was breathless, and I explained – fully. "Oh, Mothuur!" she cried, "well, you can't keep them." "But, what could I do," I asked, ever blunt and to the point. Joy said, "Give 'em back." I explained that the Derrs had returned to their home in Lebanon, so I was stuck with my "free gift." "For heaven's sake, get them out of the attic – it's unsanitary – they get fleas or something," she said. And with this admonition she rang off, thoroughly ticked off with my carelessness. I was alone once more with the intruders.

Next day, Tuesday, I rang Beris in England for advice. On a rising note of hysteria, he said, "What? How many? where?" I heard my son, Steve, ask, "What has she done now?" and Beris replied, "She's got six chickens in the attic!" I heard shrieks of laughter and I became quite indignant and retorted that Steve shouldn't laugh so heartily. A man his age could get a hernia – if his mother didn't get him first.

After some very unhelpful remarks from England, like, "I've heard of bats in the belfry – but chickens in the attic – oh, Mother, you've got 'em both," I rang off quite miffed, and determined that, right or wrong, I would cope.

And by St. George I did! Within five days I had my new pets settled into the tool shed after utilizing the extra large air travel box that our biggest dog had flown in from Africa. At one end it had a dog door that latched, and the other end was covered with wire mesh. Jim Derr, our ever-helpful neighbour, strung a heavy electrical cable thro' the trees and into the tool shed,
where I hooked up an inspection drop light to give some safe heat.

Before long, I had moved the dog box-hen house out to the side of the shed, made a small run, and watched my chicks grow. They grew so fast, and soon I was able to discern that I had three hens and three roosters. Unfortunately for the "fellas," their fate was sealed. After I fed them up well, the "gentlemen" ended up roosting in Anna Beauchamp's freezer. So I was left with three hens. One hen got sickly and got the chop, so now the count was down to two: a big Rhode Island Red named "Big Momma," and a little black and white speckled hen I called "Mrs. Fluffyknickers." They faithfully provide me with an egg each, daily.

There are many humourous stories to tell of my struggles to house and rear "the gift," but they must wait until another day. The reason for "the gift," you ask? To occupy me during my enforced separation from my husband. It worked wonderfully – great psychotherapy!

Over time my name as a "Chicken – Whisper" became "universal"—So much so that one year after the State Fair was finished I was cajoled into fostering six more hens that were refugees from an intensive FFA project abandoned by some careless teens who didn't manage to win a trophy.

The new birds were an exotic colorful tribe of Israel being two or three different make/shapes and sizes, some were quite strange looking. None the less I amalgamated the "newbies" into my flock and proceeded to name them all.

One tall long necked fowl sported a tuft of white feathers upon it's head that waved with abandon with her nervous jerky movements – She became Priscilla.

One wonderful sight was "The Egyptian" whose Feathers seemed to grow in bands of black and gold – so eye catching. A small black speckled hen, a chunky little thing who hustled everywhere became "The Bully". All of them got some type of recognition and in time we became friends, mainly because I was the provider. But my longtime residents were quite perturbed by my foisting upon them without warning or councilling, such a "circus act". So the "circus crowd" spent quite a few dark lonely nights in the pen, not comfy and warm in the hen house. But time and proximity prevailed and soon all was as I wanted it to be – no fights except of course for "The Bully" who pestered everyone, I know you must have met someone similar at some time.

"Big Momma" continued to be regal, calm and good mannered, but she was boss and little "Mrs. Fluffy knickers" was her 2nd I.C. – her wingman always. Her wingman, at her elbow as it were?

Over our time I always thanked momma and Mrs. Fluffy knickers when they laid me an egg – "Thank you ladies" or "Thank you madam" I would say as I picked up the offering. A little spoken appreciation goes a long way to smooth ruffled feathers and to foster productivity in hens. – (and workers) Soon Momma had vetted the "Circus" newcomers so her house was put in order and everyone slept together from then on.

Sometimes I let "Momma" out to free range and she has thoroughly cowed all three cats and two dogs. Personally I think she is trying to improve her social skills – but my husband says she is a bully – pure and spiteful.

Most days when she sees me in the yard she paces up and down the wire fence like a caged tiger – with feathers – fluffing and clucking asking me to come let her out to pastures new, maybe to help me weed my new grown spring plantings – not likely lady I say. But we do have some fun when I take the garden fork to turn over a compost patch of the chicken run, so she can get her worm ration, she stands on the shoulder of the fork whilst I am digging – why? – She gets a first view of emerging worms and the first serving. – golly she was fast!

In time I gained enough skill to keep 'em all cackling away and laying the occasional egg for me.

The original reason for my gift was so kind and thoughtful and I gained a lot of individual good hen type buddies from it. (and readers I hope)

OH, MY!

Easter Sunday was nearly over. My husband and I returned home from our neighbors' family gathering tired but very happy with our day. We changed into work clothes; stock must be fed and watered, eggs collected, the evening chores of small time homesteaders. I put on a tee shirt and shorts.

Last week we had moved the "hotwire" fence allowing the sheep and cattle to browse on a patch of weeds and brush. The hen house was now within the circle of the live wire and I needed access to it so I could cater to my feathered friends. Beris knew that the fence made me nervous and the turn-off switch is 'way down the hill,' so he made a plan for me to get over the live wires.

There are two strands of wire. I unscrew the upper yellow plastic conductor that holds the top wire, slide it down the upright rebar until it meets the bottom yellow plastic conductor, take a firm turn on the screw to hold it down, and step daintily over the two wires. Easy, ain't it?

The cattle are so nosy, they investigated the chickens, their run, and the hen house, and in the process they left numerous calling cards, so I walked carefully when I went to check for eggs. Recognizing me as the source of occasional treats, the sheep arrived at the gallop; they crowded around me pushing and shoving against my legs clamoring noisily for tidbits. I have to push and shove back to keep my balance; if set to music my gyrations might become the latest cha-cha craze.

Despite the aggravation, I managed to give the hens a handful of corn and picked up two lovely new-laid eggs. Turning from the hen house, carefully cupping the two eggs in my hand, I encountered the ewe who was the most pushy of the bunch. Slickly, I sidestepped her – stepping into a very lush, day-old cowpat. My rubber-shod foot slid away at increasing speed, thus enabling me to execute an <u>almost</u> perfect ballet type exercise. Possibly, it was nothing that had ever been attempted in ballet history, and such are the rules of gravity, not to mention the laws of Murphy, that I managed to alight on the very cowpat that had caused my gymnastics in the first place.

Whilst in midair, my hand must have gone into spasm and gooey, crunchy stuff was oozing out between the fingers of my right fist – you're right – two new-laid eggs! Staggering up the slope to the electric fence that was still in the lowered position inviting me to just step over, I clutched shakily at the top of the upright rebar to steady myself, lifted my right leg over the wires – then in a split second I heard an ominous Brrrrrup – it was the yellow plastic conductor zipping up that bar straight for me carrying a live wire.

The fence has now been moved!!

Breakfast in Bed

I keep chickens – only a few, the first set were a gift – a hopeful psychological panacea for what had ailed me at the time. But that is another story.

Now I *like* my chickens, not love them, but sort of like them. Sometimes they can become a pain, especially on mornings of snow, frost or rain. That is when my ambition to be a "lady farmer, U.S.A. style," starts to wane. But I do have a sense of responsibility and do right by them. Well, mostly!

They don't always rise at the proverbial "cockcrow," dawn, because they have to be released from the hen house and I definitely do not rise at dawn.

One Sunday as we were leaving church, a friend enquired how I was "coping with my chickens." Imagine my expression when a neighbour's voice piped up, "Lyn Brickles has the most spoiled, best-fed chickens in the county – she feeds them breakfast in bed – *hot* breakfast in bed!"

I couldn't think why that statement should be a source of amusement? But it was, judging by the chuckles and remarks of the bystanders – at my expense. Penny proceeded to inform them that I cook up scraps and peelings in the mornings and feed them to my chickens.

So, what is wrong with that? After all, I was a novice at this game. My only guidelines to poultry raising came out of a book borrowed from Silverton Library, and a few vaguely-remembered bits and pieces from my father's erratic period of fowl husbandry on a small holding in Buckinghamshire, England.

The library book had been published in 1942, practically the "year one." Besides, it was completely beyond my comprehension. So, I dredged thro' the cold grey ashes of my memory, and slowly brought forth some facts.

Daddy *did* feed his fowls hot meal in the mornings! And he was a successful poultry farmer in his own small way. I'm talking 1933-34 here – Depression was Lord. You prayed a lot, did what you could, and ate *sparingly.*

Dad's outdoor kitchen was a very large, black, iron cauldron perched atop a fierce fire in a makeshift brick fireplace down by the hen runs. There, he would boil up old spoiled vegetables, table scraps, and fish heads and entrails – phew! What a stink! My throat automatically closes at the memory. All this was done outside because there was *no way* my mother was going to allow that reeking mess in *her* house.

After a good boiling, Dad would pour poultry meal into the hot mess, mix it up, ladle it into buckets, and head for the chicken runs. I remember still, the commotion that his arrival caused. From all directions on the one and one-half acre paddock would come hens, ducks, and geese, their necks stretched out like bargain hunters at the after-Christmas sales, running with their funny, stiff-legged, high kicking gaits, their fluffy knickered bottoms wobbling from side to side, and all those different throats calling, "Me first – me first!"

Suddenly, with an air like royalty, thro' the crowd, through this heaving mass of dust, feathers, and screeching cries, would strut "Roger the Dodger." He did not need to hurry. He was secure in the knowledge that he was the supreme being. The choicest morsels, the largest share, also every hen in sight were his by right.

"Roger the Dodger" was a very large, beautifully-plumaged rooster – he was King of the Heap, Big Daddy, the Top Man – and he was *mean*. Not just pecking and chasing mean – Roger went for the kill! On people, he went for the face and eyes, his dangerous spurs raked and marked other fowl and dogs who made the mistake of invading his domain. With his curved, yellow beak and spurs on his heels, like Turkish scimitars, he was a formidable foe.

To this day, over my right brow is the scar from being attacked, when six years old, by that darn cockerel. My dad had to take a pitchfork to Roger to rescue me, covered in gore, from the field. My mother's pleas, added to my piercing shrieks, could not move my father to turn executioner and give Rog' the chop. The bird's proven virility was much too valuable, and I'm sure Dad had high hopes that I would stop yelling eventually.

Anyway, how to catch him? Why do you think he was called "Roger the Dodger?" One-on-one, he could mix and match all comers, on two legs or four.

Eventually, of course, Roger got his in spades!! One fine day Dad was down in the paddock scything off the lush leaves and digging up the roots of a patch of wild horseradish so that mother could make her famous horseradish sauce. Mother and I watched from the other side of the fencing, still very wary of Roger. Dad leaned the spade against the wire fence with the other tools, and knelt to pick out the roots and put them in the wheelbarrow next to him.

That's when Roger attacked, beak, spurs, wings, and all. Dad went down and Roger would not let go. Mother ran thro' the gate, all fear forgotten. She grabbed the first handle she saw, and, as Roger flew up in the air to renew his attack on Dad, she swung – a mighty, heaving swing – and decapitated Rog' in mid air. She had picked up the scythe!

For a minute it seemed to rain blood over all of us, then Daddy looked up, scratched and bleeding over face, neck, and arms, he pointed at the open gate and shouted, "Evelyn, you've let the bloody hens out!"

Foolhardy at the best of times, Dad had forgotten that Mom still held the scythe whilst she gazed fascinated as Roger did a macabre, headless dance. Finally, he fell over onto the red-sploshed, green horseradish leaves in a twitching heap. So, sometimes, are the mighty fallen, at the hands of unthinking courage.

Mother quietly leaned the handle of the scythe once more against the fence, gave my father a long, hard stare whilst her fingertips gave tiny strokes to the wooden handle she had just relinquished. "So, Paddy," she softly replied, "they are your hens – you get them in!"

She turned on her heel, strode out of the paddock – leaving the gate open – took my hand in hers, and then passed, straight-backed and bloody, into the cottage to wash up.

It was quite strange – no one spoke of "Roger the Dodger" again – nor of the way in which he had met his end. I suppose that might be called a tacit agreement!

Old Sayings – New Tricks

Just like riding a bike! What a turn up for the book! A bit over the top! He knows the ropes! Never too old to learn! Sayings, catch phrases, slogans, blessings – all are part of our language and we take them for granted (as a rule).

I have been thinking over one old saying that was very apt for a situation I had found myself part of last year.

I can always tell a long story and rather than shorten it I'll tell it long.

Our daughter Joy breeds meat goats and one of her Does needed to be put out to grass. So we ended up with "Wendy" for her retirement in our paddock. (1 Goat)

But Wendy was lonely, fretting and off her food – she missed the herd and as a result Wendy's last daughter – Mavis and two granddaughters came to stay with us. (4 Goats).

The girls settled down with Grandma and chewed away to their hearts delight, the paddock became less scruffy and all was calm and well.

To me all goats – he and she alike – look to be in a terminal state of pregnancy, but we gradually became aware the expanding girth of young Mavis was not entirely due to over eating!

So this was a right turn up for the for the books! It seems that our girl had sneaked under the curtain before she left home, got nailed and was indeed pregnant.

Beris was pleased because now the goats were more interesting and he had experience with lambing whilst still a "Local Yokel" in Lincolnshire farming country, so he knew all the ropes – just like riding a bike!

I'm not saying Mavis had our full attention but Beris spruced up the goat barn and put in a separate section – making a sort of a "birthing suite". No – I do not mock – he did a good job. Then he watched and waited for certain signs of impending presentation.

Personally the saga did not touch me, I was aware in my brain's "Dump Box" that Beris was involved with caring about Mavis's condition and keeping her well, but he assured me he was "up" on the subject and I gratefully left all the anticipation in his capable hands.

UNTIL THE NIGHT OF FEBRUATY 13TH 2009 The expectant Uncle "B" had been maundering about since midday watching the goats rear end for "signs" – I thought it was a bit over the top – I knew it was her first kid but "Really".

Snug in bed and reading, I was insulated from what was going on in the goat barn. But not for long. My Beris came in wearing his outer gear to ask for my help. The kid was very large and not well presented – Mavis needed help and after attempting to help her he needed me to use my smaller hands to move the young ones head.

Now let's hold up here, apart from my own Babes I had never seen animals give birth. So a nervous novice vet with jeans and a sweat shirt pulled over my Jammies stumbled out into the cold February night and nervously entered a poorly lit "Birthing suite" where Mavis was making a great deal of noise trying to give birth.

Dear Lord don't let me do it wrong I thought as I knelt in the great pillows of straw Beris had built up. Eventually with a great deal of effort on Mavis's part a very large male kid was delivered and I rubbed his face clean with an old towel we had stacked in there.

I still knelt in the straw because although I had put the kid to her Mavis was not at all interested in him.

All the time this drama was taking place Grandma Wendy and "the Aunties" were peering over the partition noisily jumping up and down on each others backs to see what was going on, making more noise than Mavis and acting like "Looky Loos" on a trip. I don't know if they were scolding me for the bad things they thought I was doing to Mavis – or was it advice?

Let's face it when you are up to your elbows in a mucky situation everybody becomes as expert. The new baby was shivering and so I rubbed him with a towel because he was still wet all over and I was a little worried that Mavis would not let me push the kid to her, in my total ignorance of animal midwifery it seemed natural for her to clean him. I reached out to Mavis and she gave a sudden lurch toward me – I recoiled and still on my knees in the straw I had no room to move away. Then I shouted "there's another one" and carried on a wave of birthing fluid a tiny goat baby landed on my lap, soaking me to the skin. Quickly I rubbed his face clean and realized that dear Mavis was still in labour when I was trying to get her to see to No. 1.

Now we had two baby boys and the fans in the gallery were still doing the cheer leading thing.

After a lot of cleaning up and settling Mavis down with her twins we put my clothes in the Washer and me in the bath, then a nice cuppa tea. (6 Goats). I was on a high – I couldn't come down – I was a goat midwife inducted by baptism by flood and it was St. Valentines day!!

Like they say "You're never too old to learn a new trick".

SOME SORT OF A CHRISTMAS STORY!

"Christmas is coming – the goose is getting fat" and there is an intruder in our hen house!

How do I know? For a start a week ago I found the water bottles lying on the floor and ominously one had a long smear of blood on it. Further evidence was the many black feathers on the straw and after inspecting the four hens I found that the little black one was limping, she had a nasty wound on one leg.

I puzzled over these events, finally deciding that "Big Red Momma", the matriarch of my little brood, was not to blame this time. I know "Momma" for a bully but the black chook's wound was too severe to have been inflicted by a beak.

So what? and when? – when was clearly the night before – so what?

Two days later I discovered a tunnel opening up into the hen house from under the tool shed, the hen house is a lean to-built against the lee wall of the tool shed. I blocked the mouth of the tunnel with a board on which I stood two of the filled gallon water jugs.

Next day the varmint had by-passed my amateur road block and another hole gaped up at me. Aha! A challenge!

Now the hen house is a true "Heath Robinson" lean to with an earth floor, built before my dear hubby had perfected his skills as an owner of rural property, but aided most kindly by amused helpful and skilled country friends and neighbors he has become honed to a fine tilth! and does not like to be reminded of past follies – like makeshift hen houses!!

Anyway by now I was a tiny bit annoyed by my foe, my "Irish" was up, the red dander flag was raised and I scoured the area for the means to thwart this challenger – whatever it was!

A piece of rigid, small mesh fencing about a yard square seemed to be the answer, so I hammered it under the edge of the tool shed inside the hen house, anchored it with a lump of heavy metal and three one gallon water jugs.

As an afterthought I scouted the perimeter of the tool shed.

I did wonder if my behavior was becoming obsessive, like prison warders whose charges escape thru' tunnels, could mine be the reverse?

Four entry holes easily marked by the mounds of excavated earth around them, were soon filled with lengths of metal pipe and logs, every effort accompanied by a muttered cussword from my delicate lips, lips that by now were stretched into a thin line as I thought of the cheekiness of my foe.

My husband returned from one of his business trips, listened patiently to my outraged recital, and, as his way, he reassured me that "he would fix it"- famous last words, for now failure has got to him as well, but he has deduced that this little beast is feasting nightly on the chicken meal in the dispenser hanging in the hen house and that it digs a new tunnel every night!

We have not had any eggs for ten days now, is our intruder taking them as well? Is it a raccoon? a fox? a gopher?, Can't be skunk 'cos we would smell it.

Some of the remedies our circle of friends and relatives have advanced as solutions for our problem have been pretty gross, but we went ahead and scooped out the mucky cat litter and deposited it with dog doo doo into the tunnels – to no avail. I think the chickens were holding their noses, as we were, but our nemesis was undeterred.

Then Saturday last, in the dark, Beris opened the hen house door with flashlight beaming and surprised a young skunk with his hand in the "cookie jar". No wonder the odors we created didn't work!

Isn't it strange how all those friendly purveyors of outlandish advice and tacky instructions become instantly less than helpful when you say "skunk". Through guffaws of "better you than me buddy" and laughter, all we got was "it's your problem baby", and "we must be calm".

This morning I went down to let out the hens as I usually do and that pest had tipped out all the meal from the container and it lay on the floor in a soiled heap.

"That's it" I shouted and threw everything out of the place, I had to wedge open the door because we have a gale force wind blowing today and it kept slamming it shut leaving me inside in the dark. After finding more rigid fencing I renewed my efforts on the floor and short of reinforced concrete I felt it would do the job.

I placed a heavy straw filled chest and other heavy gear on top and moved the nesting boxes, in which lay one egg, the first for about ten days. After surveying my hard work I tidied up, took the container and refilled it with meal and placed it outside under cover.

Remembering the solitary egg I went back into the hen house and the wind promptly slammed the door shut behind me, but I knew where the egg was located so I stretched out my hand into the nest box.....and the back of my hand touched something warm and fluffy!!....in an instant my skunk programmed brain flashed an alarm that cried "Skunk – Skunk – Skunk" and I yelled – loud!

Then a hen exploded from the nest box in flurry of feathers and piercing "I'm in trouble" type hen shrieks. Now let's face it she wasn't the only one in there who was scared, I had trouble in hanging on to more than my wits. After that I lost it – I really lost it! I stalked around the back of the tool shed – two more holes were winking at me and on the impulse of a frightened fool I picked up a can of kerosene and sloshed the stinking stuff all around the edges of the shed, "get on with that stink Skunk" I shouted.

Back in my kitchen with my solitary egg and a cup of coffee, sanity slowly returned and I thought, "all I need is for the blasted skunk to take umbrage and find a box of matches"!

My husband, appalled at my stupidity found a trapper, a nice young man who set traps on Christmas Eve and dispatched my nemesis on Christmas Morning.

I guess the moral of this story is – send for the trapper sooner!!

The Strangeness of Being a Stranger

To place my tale – I should tell that Beris and I make haphazard day trips to the Coast when we can, and always we vary our routes.

One favourite ride is on route R.34 from Corvallis to Waldport – (you can get great Fish and Chips in Waldport) and on the way the tiny old hamlet of Alsea always attracts my interest – especially an almost "Oregon Trail" antique style of "General Store."

My inquisitive mind asks what kind of treasures are hidden in corners inside?

I guess I must say it aloud because usually Beris, parks the car and says – "take your time Hunny" and I go browsing –I am blessed.

I had entered the store and looked around, "help ya maam". I turned, a young man stood just behind me, obviously he had offered to help me and was waiting for my reply. So I trotted out my stock phrase – "Thank You, But I Am Just Browsing." No sooner had I spoken when his casual, languid manner changed. His face became blank and he scrutinized me as tho' I wore a sign saying – "Shoplifter Here".!!!

"If ya need help maam just you holler" he said as he walked toward the back of the store, but still continuing to stare strangely at my face, not a smile nor a tic, did he show as he retreated. Soo'oh!! I did browse – but maybe not quite as casually as I did before.

I had a slow stroll up and down the many aisles of goods in what was obviously a Dry Goods Store, aside from a wide range of groceries, they carried chains for trucks and heavy oil in large red jugs, rope for lariats, gum boots, horse blankets, cowboy shirts for him and her – so much stuff.

Not my style of treasure, but interesting and defiantly a "General Store", not antique. Passing a refrigerator I remembered that in the area was a known Goat Cheese maker, so I looked in the fridge but had no luck

As I closed the door "the helper" was to hand – beside me no less.

Strangely his demeanor had changed – a smile was bestowed on me and I was asked again – could this (transformed) young man help me.

I took a deep breath and told of my search in vain for Goat Cheese, upon my words he showed me the goodies I had been unable to find myself. And to serve me further he gave me a very interesting resume on the many types of cheese made locally.

Finally I made my way to the till to pay for my cheese, and after waiting until the 2 young lady cashiers had decided upon what type of dangly earings would suit them best I took my small purchase and left the General Store.

Beris had parked at the side of the building and as I walked around to the car I noticed my "helper" reentering thro' a large side door, he smiled and waved a hand as he disappeared inside.

Beris was chuckling as I sat down, he told me that "my helper" had come out to talk to him – he told my husband that I was inside "browsing" and Beris told him that I did that a lot, it was the buying that worried him.

The "helper" and my husband had a conversation that depending on your mood/attitude can almost be an interrogation, people are interested in strangers. I related what I felt about "my helpers" manner inside the store and then as "ONE" we said – "it was the accent"!!

We are mostly unaware of the difference, but some times folks will go into a sort of fugue state, as they get you to speak.

It's a gift, we meet the nicest people and make friends, and laugh a lot.

MY HUSBAND HAS A MERRY HEART. Prov. 17:22

I Had A Dream – (Truly)

Some weeks ago I had a dream – So vivid that when I awoke I wrote it down as follows:

In my dream I was taking part in a writing class held in a barn like structure and the young lady teacher set an "item project" – she handed separate items – all different – to each member of the class. When it was my turn she led me to a bench by the door, picked up a small burlap sack, hefted it toward me and said "take this sack of sand to the park, come back in 1½ hrs. with a story to read to us."

This was my project!!? O.K. Try it out for size – 2 lbs of sand dragged at my poor old arthritic elbow joint as I stood "Duh" holding the sack. The teacher pointed at the door and then at her watch.

Finally my brain engaged and I stumbled out of the hall and walked along the street toward the small town park. "What a crock" I thought – what can you say about sand that would be interesting? Sitting on the first bench I came to I ran scenarios through my mind trying to find a spark of inspiration.

Beach Sand – tell of the bright white sand on the beaches of the southern coast of South Africa that are lapped by the Indian Ocean – or – of the dirty red sand of the Kalahari Desert – NAH!

I moved along toward the small wooden band – stand in the centre of the park – dragging my burden with me and sat on the steps leading up to the platform.

Sand Castles – No – that's back to beaches. Sand Timer/Hour Glass – yes time is flying and I've only got 1 ½ hrs to write something – even less time now.

Should I make shift a tray and try to write in the sand as I did in "the olden days" – I don't think so.

A sand shoe shuffle would maybe awaken my brain but probably would be more than my ancient knees could manage with any style.

Moving away from the Band Stand back toward the Hall I thought of – Sand Paper and Quick Sand – where most of my creative brain cells felt buried. I knew I had failed my "Item Project" and as I returned to enter the class I realised I had also lost the sack of sand!!!

Of all the people in the class reading the end result of their "Item Projects" I had even lost the sand – over time.

I was a failure with NO STORY TO READ.

And Then Perhaps Not!!

Was there a reverse story here.

BREATHING

It's all in the breathing – deep relaxing breathing.

After all wasn't it our first deep breath that – with a blessing – launched us into this life?

So take a deep breath – step outside barefoot onto night damp planks, feel the chill of an early April morning and see the sun as it climbs over the uneven fringe of tall trees in the forest. See how the sun's rays anoint, to sparkle like crystal, the drops of moisture on leaves and grass.

Feel warm furry bodies wrap around your bare ankles in greeting and anticipation of breakfast.

Take another breath and slowly let it go – and another, you are a whole being.

Focus on sensation and movement, give yourself to the movement, the breathing – the search for a place.

Soon a sense of inner quiet filters into your psyche – almost other—worldly in essence and so peaceful.

But breathe – move slowly and surely along a learned pattern. The sense of achievement is sweet tasting and soothing – and breathe.

Follow the pattern and you can be renewed and so find your own sense of place – anywhere – for it is inside of you all the time.

So to continue the journey – Take a deep breath, Whisper "Hallelujah"

SERENDIPITY

Serendipity is the faculty of making fortunate and unexpected discoveries by accident.

I'm sure that many folks have at some time suffered illness that seemed reluctant to let go.

In such circumstances sometimes the spirit becomes dimmed and your faith takes a beating despite your prayers.

Here is part of the story of my climb back, an acknowledgment that caring is part of the cure, the best medicine.

Rest they said, rest – so I rested, sheltered under a fleecy blanket on the sofa by the window. I watched a blizzard grow from single lazy flakes to a whirling dervish of wind and particles. Snow settled over the flower beds and tiny green spears of newly birthed daffodils until they too were covered by a fleecy blanket. And I slept.

When next I opened my eyes all was quiet outside, the storm had passed and left a white world, at peace, unblemished.

I was so cozy and comfy I felt as sumptuous as a piece of warm buttered toast on a lovely blue plate.

Then appeared two loving hands bearing a cup of tea – to place next to my blue plate.

Serendipity!!

God is good. Amen.

AMBITION/ONE STEP AT A TIME

The sound of a car door slamming shut made me glance out of the kitchen window, there I saw my 16 year old grandson, Frank, bouncing along the path to the back door.

Topping a painfully skinny body, his tousled, blonde head jerked back and forth to the beat of a drummer only he could hear.

Draped over his bony frame was a fashionable overlarge Tee shirt, the logo of which displayed advertising for his idols the Blazers Basketball team.

Tight purple Lycra cycle pants overlaid with a skimpy pair of baby blue soccer shorts encased his lower torso. Long spaghetti-thin legs, almost shapeless, except for lumpy knobs where knees would someday, hopefully, develop, were grounded in large, clumpy black sport boots and a pair of long, grubby socks fought, in differing degrees, a losing battle with gravity.

The back door clunked shut and Frank breezed in, "Hi, Gramma, how ya doin'?" he greeted me and enveloped me in an awkward half hug, almost embarrassed to be hugging a female, even a Gramma. He was at that stage in his social development where showing affection or caring might be viewed as sissy, but his Dad hugged me so he may have felt that it was all right . . . but he wouldn't have done it in public.

A waft of the frosty November air hung around his along with a frisson of excitement, obviously he had something to tell but I hung back from asking outright, instead I asked, "Would you like some soup and toast, Frankie?" – oops – I had forgotten that the IE on the end of his given name was now taboo, also part of the development stage.

"Gramma, please don't call me Frankie, it's so babyish, My name is Frank."

"Sorry, Frank," I apologized, "do you want soup and toast?"

"Yes, please Gramma and no butter on the toast," he said and seated himself, with a great deal of chair scraping and table rocking from those long, awkward legs.

I filled a bowl with my good veggie soup and along with a couple pieces of toast – unbuttered – and placed his meal in front of him.

As he spooned up soup and munched toast, I inquired after his parents, my son, Steve, and his wife, Rhoda. If I expected some detailed information on their situation and health I was disappointed. "Oh, they're OK," was all I got.

So I asked, "How is work at the store?" This was in reference to Frank's past time job after school and holiday time, filling shelves at a local super market. He made pocket money for gas to run his car and a little more to buy the occasional piece of clothing to keep himself in fashion. Items that Rhoda and Steve might balk at buying for him, on the grounds that it was either cheap or ugly – or both.

"Oh, the job is good, "he replied," and I've been promoted." So this is why he seemed so excited – PROMOTION – WOW – I hadn't realized he was ambitious in this work area, but I gave him my full beam approval along with exclamations of delight, praising his industry in achieving this honor so young.

I asked to what exalted position he had been elevated – Counter Clerk, Supervisor? – Assistant Manager? – He started to rise from the table, causing the same minor havoc as before – but in reverse – saying his lunch hour was nearly over and he must get back to the store. He was to begin his training period this afternoon.

"for what?" I almost screeched.

"Oh, didn't I tell you, Gram, I'm being upgraded, Packer and Carryout, after my training."

I was stunned. This was promotion? But I hid my consternation and made appropriate noises and small comments to him as he headed toward the back door.

"Bye, Gramma," he said, "thanks for the soup . . . gotta get back to the job."

"Bye, Frank . . . well done and good luck!"

He left, as he came . . . carried on the crest of a wave of sureness in his own abilities.

I thought . . . "I love you, Frankie, and I just know you'll go far . . . God Bless you, lad."